UNDER THE
YARMULKE

Yarmulke: a small circular cover for the head worn by Jewish men, especially at religious ceremonies

Cambridge International Dictionary of English

UNDER THE
YARMULKE

TALES OF FAITH, FUN AND FOOTBALL

RABBI SOLOMON SCHIFF

CHAI BOOKS

Under the Yarmulke
Tales of Faith, Fun and Football
By Rabbi Solomon Schiff

Published by Chai Books
Miami, Florida
www.undertheyarmulke.com

Copyright © 2011 by Solomon Schiff

Library of Congress Catalog Card Number: 2011960036

ISBN: 978-1-4664989-0-7

Interior Design by 1106 Design
Cover Design by Bruce Kluger
Photos courtesy of Solomon Schiff

For Shirley

Table of Contents

Foreword

I CAN CLOSE MY EYES even now and hear Sol Schiff's powerful, mellifluous voice as he chanted the beautiful words of the Hebrew prayer book. I remember feeling that there was something heroic in the boldness with which he proclaimed the spiritual truths contained in our tradition. It inspired me to love my Judaism more profoundly and be committed to it more deeply. But there was much more about Rabbi Schiff that makes him so unique.

The synagogue rabbi is the infantry soldier of the Jewish people. His job is often not glamorous. He must regularly put up with a demanding and fractious board. His monetary compensation and moral support from the community are usually inadequate. But he is the pivot around which the Jewish community revolves. With dedicated and determined communal rabbis, Judaism flourishes, families congregate, and youth are inspired. With lackluster rabbis who merely call it in, the synagogues are empty and the Jewish people are impoverished.

To be an effective shule rabbi is to respond to a calling rather than a career. It means fundamentally subordinating one's ego to a cause much larger than oneself. It requires daily sacrifice and eternal selflessness. The rabbi gets up at the crack of dawn to lead services seven days a week. He must prepare fiery sermons that excite the congregation. He must then shift gears and softly pitch Bar Mitzvah boys on the meaning of becoming a young man. He must counsel married couples in crisis. He must lend confidence to those who have lost their way. And he must provide comfort to ravaged individuals suffering catastrophic loss.

No job is more demanding of every facet of our human talents and every emotion of the heart. But amid all this, the rabbi must not overlook the needs of his own family who are his principal responsibility.

From my earliest years, I witnessed Rabbi Solomon Schiff perform all of these duties (and more) as he became an extraordinary rabbi, husband, and father. As rabbi of the Hebrew Academy school, where I was a student from the age of eight, Rabbi Schiff inspired thousands of young students while caring for the elderly members of the community with patience and compassion. I saw him hold together a synagogue through good times and challenging days.

But those were not his only obligations. As executive vice president of the Rabbinical Association of Greater Miami, the community's welfare was his first concern. And among his vast responsibilities, he never tired and never waned.

However, there is a personal dimension to my relationship with Rabbi Schiff. His son, Steven, was my classmate for many years. I played in the Schiff home after school. I watched TV in his living room. I joined the family for supper. I actively remember the love and caring Rabbi Schiff always showed his children.

As a rabbi, I can attest to how challenging it is to come home, after a long day of communal obligations, and offer one's children the time and involvement they require. But Rabbi Schiff's children were the apple of his eye, and the warm and loving atmosphere he and his wife, Shirley, created will be forever embedded in my memory.

Under the Yarmulke is a wonderful collection of stories that will inspire, teach, and entertain as only Rabbi Schiff can do.

Rabbi Shmuley Boteach

Introduction

ONCE UPON A TIME, after the first service I ever conducted as a new rabbi in Dubuque, Iowa, a woman approached me with a compliment.

"Rabbi, I loved your sermon. It was short but brief."

"Thank you," I said. "I'll take that as a compliment." She shrugged and headed toward the refreshments. I was left holding my tongue, so to speak, somewhat embarrassed.

Years later, I was invited to participate in an interfaith panel at a luncheon meeting in Miami. As I opened the door to enter, I realized that I had forgotten my jacket. I hesitated to come into the room, and Reverend Calvin Rose, a Protestant minister who was one of the panelists, must have noticed how befuddled I was by the situation. He approached me gently.

"Sol, why don't you come in?" he asked.

"I forgot my jacket," I said, "I'm embarrassed to go inside. All the men are wearing jackets."

Calvin coaxed me inside and urged me to join him at the podium. He approached the microphone and said, "These meetings are too darn formal. I don't know about you, but I'm taking off my jacket."

All the men immediately stood up and removed their jackets. It was a perfect moment. This sensitive, thoughtful, and good-humored clergyman taught that audience a lesson that was much more effective than any sermon he could have given; namely that one must do everything one can to spare the embarrassment of a fellow human being and make him feel welcome in whatever setting presents itself.

And so it is with this book. After being a rabbi for so many years, I decided to remove my official clergyman's garb and share some anecdotes and stories with what I hope will become my expanded "congregation."

I offer them with great humility and delight. Now, if someone finds my jacket, please let me know.

1
Why a Rabbi?

I AM OFTEN ASKED when and why I decided to become a rabbi. The answer is that in the year 1942, as a teenager, my father, of blessed memory, took me to Madison Square Garden in New York. At that time there was a huge rally concerning the mass extermination of European Jewry, which was just becoming known. The Garden was overflowing, and we stood outside together with thousands of people hearing the proceedings over loudspeakers.

As we heard the impassioned speeches of prominent leaders, demanding that the United States Government intercede to stop this massacre (I don't believe the term "Holocaust" was known then), I saw my father crying for the first time in my life.

"Poppa," I asked him, "Why are you crying?"

"Shloimele," he replied gently. "They are talking about our mishpocha, our family. We have brothers, sisters, nephews, nieces, uncles, and aunts, about eighty in all, that are being exterminated. Many of our family members are rabbis and leaders of their communities."

"Don't worry, Poppa," I said, with real conviction. "When I grow up, I will become a rabbi to take their place."

It was in front of Madison Square Garden, in 1942, that I decided to become a rabbi. As the years unfolded, and the massive extermination of six million of our Jewish brothers and sisters became known, I became more convinced that I had an obligation to try to make up, in my own limited way, for the tremendous loss of our people.

Many years later, after one of the first sermons I ever gave as an ordained rabbi, a woman complimented me (I think) by saying, "Rabbi, I loved your sermon. It was short, but brief." Even then, flush with the new responsibility of addressing a congregation, I knew that actions spoke louder than words and that sermons alone would never prevent another Holocaust. Still inspired by my childhood experience with my father, I was determined to do much more than simply talk... and talk...and talk.

A rabbi should lead by example, as in keeping kosher, both at home and away. But this can present the possibility of real embarrassment, should the rabbi ever stray from his appointed path as a man of the cloth.

I was once called to a Veterans Hospital and asked to take a blood test as part of an experiment. The burn unit was doing an experiment on burn victims. The biggest problem with burn victims is that when the skin is destroyed, the fluids ooze out, causing severe damage. They were experimenting with pigskin, which they believed was the closest to human skin. The problem was that anyone tested who had eaten pig meat would have built up immunity. They figured that an Orthodox rabbi, who never ate pig, would not have built up any immunity.

As the technician was about to draw the blood, he stopped.

"Rabbi, I want to warn you, if you ever ate anything from a pig, it will show up in your blood."

What do I do? To back down would imply that I had eaten pig products at some time. On the other hand, to go through with it might reveal that I had in fact ingested pig at some time. Either choice could be a huge embarrassment.

"I'll take my chances," I told him.

A few days later, the technician called to tell me I had passed.

"I guess you have nothing to worry about," he said. "If you stay on the straight and narrow."

It's a funny phrase, to "stay on the straight and narrow." I feel as if my life has been full of crazy zigzags and that it has been anything but narrow, both in vision and in practice. But in spite of all the wonderful experiences and privileges being a rabbi has brought, my reason for choosing this path always comes back to that day in 1942 when my father and I first learned about what would later be called the Holocaust. And this theme has remained constant throughout my life, from my childhood to my first pulpit, and all the way through my wonderful years in Miami, Florida.

But certain events stand out that have reignited my commitment to making the world a better place for the Jewish people. In 1962, I was sent by Rabbi Alexander S. Gross of the Hebrew Academy of Miami Beach to visit several Jewish communities in Venezuela and Columbia. The purpose of my visit was to recruit students for the Hebrew Academy.

During my visit, I met a number of Holocaust survivors, several of whom told me similar stories. When

World War II ended, survivors of the Holocaust began to rehabilitate their devastated lives. Many men and women lost their whole families and tried to start new ones.

A couple would come to a rabbi, asking him to marry them. The rabbi asked if they'd been married before. When they answered yes, he asked, "How did your marriage end?" When they answered that he or she died, he asked, "Do you have witnesses that they died?" When they replied, "No," he said that he could not marry them. According to the Halacha (Jewish law), one needs witnesses that a spouse died in order to be permitted to marry again.

The next day, the same couple came back to the rabbi with two witnesses who stated that they observed the death of the respective spouses. The rabbi then proceeded to marry the couple. The problem was, the couple knew that this was not true, the witnesses knew that this was not true, and the rabbi knew that this was not true because he was in the same death camp. The circumstance of these deaths was that masses of people were gassed and cremated, with no possibility of having witnesses survive to tell the story. This story was not uncommon. In order to get around the Jewish law, and in order to pick up their devastated lives, they had to create a fictitious story.

In January of 1968, an event occurred that brought to the fore a problem similar to the dilemma of the Holocaust survivors. An Israeli submarine, named the

Dakar, set sail from England to Israel. The submarine disappeared somewhere in the Mediterranean Sea. There was no trace of it. With no witnesses as to what happened, the seamen could not be declared dead. The government pressured the Rabbinate to decide the status of the lost seamen and thereby determine the status of their wives.

The rabbis, after considerable deliberations, came to an appropriate decision. There is a rabbinic axiom called, "Anan Saadie—We Are Witness." This means that certain things are so obvious that we, the world, are witnesses to these facts. For example, if the sun is shining, we can all attest to the fact that it is daytime.

Based on that rabbinic dictum, the rabbis ruled that we are all witnesses to the fact that if a ship does not set into port to replenish its provisions after a certain period of time, the people on the ship must not have survived. Subsequently, the rabbis declared that the *Dakar* seamen had died and that the wives were to be considered widows with all the rights and benefits entitled to them.

It would seem that following the tragedy of the Holocaust the leading rabbis of that time could have taken an alternative approach. Had they followed the principle of "where there is a will, there is a way" and invoked the axiom of "Anan Saadie," they could have declared all those in the various death camps as dead, thereby allowing the surviving spouses to legally marry and pick up the few remaining pieces of their shattered lives. This would have spared them the painful guilt that so many suffered from and enabled them to live out their remaining years with peace of mind.

The irony of these struggles has stayed with me. It continues to influence my judgment as I settle disputes within the Jewish community and offer counsel when serving on secular committees, as well.

I was fortunate once to learn a lesson in the courtroom when a friend of mine, Philip Bloom, a judge, invited me to sit with him on the bench to observe the judicial process. As he entered the courtroom, he addressed the attorneys.

"I expect all of you to behave properly. I have my rabbi sitting next to me."

After listening to many cases, a young defendant was called to the stand.

"Sol, you decide what judgment I should render in this case," my friend Philip whispered to me. I was overwhelmed with such an awesome responsibility.

"He looks like a nice young man, who probably went the wrong way," I told my friend after hearing the charges. "I think he should be let go with a warning."

The judge replied, "Okay, but first let me show you some of his history."

With that, he handed me a huge printout with almost every crime imaginable.

"Maybe you should put him away for a while," I said, which the judge did, happy that he had used better judgment than his rabbi.

So much of the world is colored in grey, and it's always a question of how we choose to interpret its varying shades. This holds true for how we perpetuate the lessons of the Holocaust. As long as we still have survivors in our midst, the Holocaust is unquestionably sacred. However, how it will remain relevant is another question altogether. Perhaps certain events, some of which I have been fortunate to witness, will answer that question by themselves, as action, once again, speaks louder than words.

On June 4, 1989, a special event was held in Miami Beach to commemorate the 50th anniversary of the S.S. *St. Louis,* the famous ship that left Hamburg, Germany, on May 13, 1939, with 937 Jewish refugees, fleeing the hell of the Holocaust. The ship was originally scheduled to dock in Havana, Cuba. However, by the time the ship crossed the Atlantic, Cuba refused to allow the ship to dock. The ship sailed along the Eastern shore of the United States and was seen by many as it passed Miami Beach. The ship's captain requested that the

United States government allow it to land on American soil. The request was denied, and the ship was forced to return to Europe, where most of the passengers were eventually exterminated.

We set sail on a small boat, which held some Holocaust survivors, including Herb Karliner, who was on the original *St. Louis,* and a number of Jewish and general community leaders. In the distance, we saw a boat anchored off the shore of the Fontainebleau Hotel. This boat had once belonged to Adolf Hitler and had been found in a junkyard in Jacksonville. Miami Beach Commissioner Abe Resnick, a Holocaust survivor and a member of our Holocaust Memorial Committee, arranged to have that vessel donated to us for use in the ceremony.

At an appointed time, someone in our boat detonated an explosive and Hitler's yacht blew up and sank, thus forming a reef, which created a positive addition to the environment. The location was most appropriate, since it was there that people lining the shore had seen the S.S. *St. Louis* several decades earlier.

The ceremony offered a symbolic message: After 50 years, Hitler and his barbarians are dead and buried and the Jewish people whom he attempted to totally annihilate are alive and well and continuing to thrive. In fact, this seemingly everlasting energy and will of the people has found a permanent place in southern Florida. In a sense, this story brings my personal experience full circle.

In the fall of 1984 in Miami Beach, a committee was formed to create a memorial for the six million Jewish victims of the Holocaust. It included several survivors, among them Dr. Helen Fagin, a professor of Holocaust studies at the University of Miami who eventually wrote the history on the memorial walls; Miami Beach Commissioner Abe Resnick; George Goldbloom; David Schaecter; Jack Chester; Ezra Katz; Harry Smith, our attorney; Kenneth Treister, a prominent local architect who created the design for the memorial; and Norman Braman, who served as our founding chairman. I have been active from the beginning on the committee and currently serve as its chairman.

The design of the memorial included a huge arm grounded in the center of the campus and stretching straight up toward the sky. Clinging to the arm were to be human-like figures of people, desperately trying to break free from the tragedy engulfing them. The memorial was also to include a reflecting pool, a wall depicting the history of European Jewry before the Holocaust, and images describing the horrors of those tragic events, with granite walls for the names of victims. The entire campus was to be made of Jerusalem stone.

When a story appeared in our local newspaper, many objected to its construction, citing the height of the arm and claiming that Miami Beach was a tourist city of sun and fun and not the right location for a memorial, which could only add a note of sadness to the atmosphere.

In response, the architect agreed to reduce the size of the memorial to a more acceptable height. The Miami Beach Commission met for its final decision as to whether it was going to allow us to build our memorial on city-owned land. Before that meeting, I spoke to a number of commissioners.

"Do you know the legal address of the site of the memorial?" I asked. "The address is 1933–1945 Meridian Avenue. The street numbers match the exact dates of the Nazi regime. For those who say this is not the right place for a Holocaust memorial, is there any place on earth with an address that is more appropriate?"

At the next meeting, the vote for granting us the location was approved unanimously. In this case, a street address was no mere coincidence. It provided the clincher to a positive argument for building the memorial exactly in the right place. For me, personally, the fact that the site was just minutes from my home became a blessing as I watched it come to life one day at a time, piece by piece and prayer by prayer.

Whenever I am asked about why I became a rabbi, I begin with the story of standing in front of Madison Square Garden with my father in 1942 and I end it with how the memorial in Miami Beach was finally finished in 1990.

Naturally, in honor of that woman who once complimented me on the success of my brief sermon, I try to keep the story short—which reminds me of another time, after another sermon, when an old woman approached me.

"Rabbi, your sermon was terrible," she said, and walked away, leaving me utterly speechless. An old man tried to console me, saying, "Rabbi, don't take her seriously; she only repeats what others say."

While attending Brooklyn College, I took a course in public speaking. Our instructor, who received her degree from a midwestern university, thought that nobody in Brooklyn knew how to speak English.

Critiquing one of my speeches, she said, "Mr. Schiff, I hope you don't choose a profession in which speaking is a part of it."

I never forgot her admonition. Rather than discourage me, it served as a strong motivator in the profession I chose as a rabbi and community leader, in which public speaking has been a fundamental ingredient.

2
A Brooklyn Boy Grows Up

M Y GRANDSON NOACH once asked me, "Zaidie, when you were growing up, did you go online?"

"Sweetheart, when I was growing up, the only thing we had on line was laundry.'"

To which he replied, "What does that mean?"

As children coming of age during the Depression, we were obsessed with making whatever money we could, in almost any way we could imagine. Since there were no parks or playgrounds for us to enjoy during the summer, we hung around our neighborhood, playing ball and waiting to get called for an errand. Very few people had telephones in their homes, so those trying to reach someone called the corner drug store. That's when we sprang into action. The druggist would find any kid available to go find the person to come to the phone. When we breathlessly informed him he had a call at the corner, we would get a tip, usually a penny or two. When we accumulated enough pennies, ten cents to be exact, we would go to the movies.

One week, my brother Morris and I eventually accumulated nineteen cents, one short of what was needed for both of us to go see a new film we were excited about. When I saw a man sitting on a porch across the street, I got an idea.

"Mister, can I ask you a question?" I said.

"Sure kid, questions are free," he replied, laughing.

"Mister, did you ever have penny trouble?" I asked.

"What's penny trouble?" he said.

"It's when you and your brother only have nineteen cents and you need one more penny to go to the movies."

He took out a shiny new penny, flipped it to me, and said, "Enjoy the movie."

As a nine year-old boy, I sang in Laskin's Choir on Atkins Avenue in Brooklyn. We practiced almost every night throughout the summer preparing for the High Holidays. I received five dollars and my older brother,

Morris, got fifteen. It wasn't because he was older; he sang solos. Another choir leader hired us to sing for Bar Mitzvahs and weddings. We had six affairs during one weekend. I noticed at the end of one wedding, the groom gave the choir leader $18. After the weekend, my brother and I went to the choir leader's house. He gave us $3 each. I told him he shortchanged us.

"What do you mean?" he asked.

I said, "I saw the man give you $18. We have six in the choir (four adults and my brother and me). That makes $3 apiece for each of the six affairs—which makes $18 for each. Between my brother and me, we should get $36."

All the men in the choir laughed. We came home. Our father was furious. A few days later, the choir leader came to the house to ask if he could hire us to join his choir for Passover. My father threw him out of the house, saying he would not let one who cheats children have anything to do with his children.

My grandson Jeremy once asked me, "Zaidie, can you tell me about your Bar Mitzvah?"

"We had religious services in the synagogue," I began, "and we invited a few friends to join us afterwards for lunch in our home."

He then asked, "When did you have the party?"

I said, "Party? That was the party."

"But when was the reception, Zaidie?"

"Jeremy, in those days, we had no reception."

His questions highlight the success and prosperity that Jews have found in America and the long way we have come from our immigrant roots.

I am on the lower right, with my father and stepmother in the middle (1940)

In fact, I had two Bar Mitzvahs. The first took place on July 8, 1942. It was a ceremony without the joy or excitement usually associated with such an important milestone. I was filled with sadness and anxiety because one of my brothers, Irving (I was the youngest of nine children), was in the army and could not get a furlough to come home. Not only was I sad that he wouldn't be with me at this most important event in my life, but I feared he might be shipped overseas.

World War II was going badly for the United States. We heard daily reports of the high casualties in the American military. This, coupled with my being aware that the Nazis were exterminating Jews all over Europe, weighed heavily on my heart. I kept thinking, what if Irving was sent to the European war zone and captured by the Germans? Would he be treated as a military prisoner, or as a Jew, with the same fate as all Jews?

Those disturbing thoughts stayed with me until November 21, 1942, when I had my second Bar Mitzvah. This date was chosen because Irving was able to get a furlough. Although I still had deep anxieties about his military future, his presence alleviated many of my fears and worries. His embrace and love was all I needed to brighten my life, even for a short while.

The story had a happy ending because the war was finished before Irving could be shipped overseas to the war zone.

As a teenager, I was involved with an organization trying to encourage youngsters in elementary Jewish day schools to go to Jewish high schools. I thought it would be very helpful if we could do a story on successful Orthodox people who had made it and were not rabbis. I would then write it up in a newsletter we put out.

I was able to reach Mr. Herman Wouk, the famous author of *The Caine Mutiny*, because he had developed a close relationship with Rabbi Moshe Feinstein, my Rebbe at the Mesifta Tifereth Jerusalem Yeshiva where I studied. As part of his life as an Orthodox Jew, Wouk had also studied with the legendary Rabbi Feinstein.

I called and made an appointment. Through some unbelievable error, I forgot about the meeting and missed my chance to meet Herman Wouk. When I realized my mistake, I wrote a multi-page letter to Mr. Wouk, apologizing for the missed appointment. I sweated out his response. Finally, it arrived. I dreaded opening his letter. As the highly skilled writer he was, he wrote back three words.

"Let's try Thursday."

I showed up for the appointment at the same place and time we had originally set up. Since I hadn't read

Mr. Wouk's best-selling book, I asked someone who had some notes about the book, so I could make an intelligent reference when I met him.

When I asked, "Do you believe that respecting authority is more important than independent thinking?" Mr. Wouk replied, "It took me eight hundred pages to answer that question."

He went on to help me do the interview by saying, "Wouldn't you like to note the books I keep on my desk?"

So I asked him, "What is the most important book you have on your desk?"

He said, "The dictionary."

I then lifted up my camera to take a photograph. As I was about to snap the picture, he said, "It will come out better if you remove the lens cap," which I did. The photo appeared with a story in our newsletter, showing him from his mouth to the top of his head.

Every boy I knew growing up in Brooklyn during this time had dreams of making money, meeting girls, and discovering the world. My close friend, Abraham Amsel, and I came up with a great idea of how to spend the summer. We were about seventeen years old and students at a Yeshiva on the Lower East Side in New York. We would apply for a job as busboys in the well-known Pioneer

Country Club Hotel in the Catskill Mountains. It sounded like an easy way not only to have a vacation, but also to enjoy the social atmosphere, including meeting girls.

Mr. Gartenberg, who owned the hotel with Mr. Schechter, conducted the job interview. Since neither of us had any experience as busboys, we concocted a sizable resume of our many experiences in the field. As we prepared to offer our resumes, Mr. Gartenberg asked, "Are you prepared to pay for every dish you break?"

We were speechless, not knowing the consequences of that question. We realized our dilemma and quickly said good-bye to Mr. Gartenberg and to our adventurous dream.

We had a similar dream of selling ice cream bars on the beach in Rockaway, New York. A third friend, Arnold Moncznik, had a great idea for making lots of money. The plan, according to his thinking, was to buy ice cream bars wholesale for a nickel apiece and sell them for a dime. The area on the beach he proposed was under no special jurisdiction of any police authority, and therefore you shouldn't need a permit to peddle ice cream. Also, we would not have to worry about competition because the area was off the beaten path.

As we began our action plan, we found that none of these suppositions were true. Every one of the points in his plan was totally wrong. Number one, the place where he recommended buying the ice cream for a wholesale price was charging not a nickel but ten cents. The selling price on the beach was ten cents, leaving us no margin for profit. Secondly, the place on the beach had signs all over saying, "No Selling Without a Permit." Finally, there were already many vendors at the beach with permits to sell ice cream. Plus, the beach police were heavily patrolling the area. Again, we had to quickly say good-bye to another adventurous dream.

My mother, Malka Feinzeig Schiff

My mother died when I was five years old. My brother Irving was the one who helped me get through this terrible time. The neighborhood kids made fun of me because I didn't cry. I don't really know why I didn't but I never forgot those kids' reaction. Nevertheless, with the strength I had managed to cultivate as the youngest of nine children, I found my way through the Depression and effectively left my neighborhood when I began attending Brooklyn College and eventually took up cantoral studies.

Brooklyn College graduate, 1946

The other day I took my grandchild Jeremy shopping to buy a pencil sharpener.

We found a small one to fit in his binder that cost $2.50.

I told him, "When I went to college, it cost $2.50 for an entire year."

He looked up at me sadly and said, "Zadie, you must've gone to a lousy school."

3

The Wild, Wild West of the Modern American Cantorate

I MADE MY DEBUT as a professional cantor in 1948, on the first night of Rosh Hashanah at the Roosevelt Synagogue on Wallace Avenue in the Bronx. There were about eight hundred worshippers in attendance and naturally I was very nervous, concentrating more on how many people were there instead of the work I was about to perform.

Before I sang a single note, my first slip came, literally, as I ascended the stairs to the pulpit in my long, ecclesiastical robe while trying to balance an especially high cantoral hat on my head. On the first stair, I stepped on my robe. As I tried to continue, my body jerked, my robe swept up, and the high hat flew off my head. I reached out and caught it before it fell.

"Good catch!" said a man in the front row. That was my first compliment. I thought I would never survive the embarrassment, but somehow I did.

I had studied all summer with the well-known Cantor Pearlman. As I was conducting the service on Rosh Hashanah, I came upon a prayer I had never seen before. I had a serious dilemma. Should I try to recite the prayer aloud and risk mistakes or should I skip it? I decided to say it silently.

After the service, a man said to me, "Cantor, you forgot to recite 'Ve Ye E Soyu.'"

"Actually, I did say it," I responded.

"I didn't hear it," he said.

"That's because I said it silently," I replied.

"By us," he said, looking somewhat unsatisfied with my answer, "we say it out loud."

"By us," I said casually, "we say it silently."

I had survived my second professional crisis. When I told this to my cantoral teacher, his response was quite encouraging.

"Son of a gun," he said, smiling broadly. "You have a good head on your shoulders."

In 1949, an ad appeared in the *Morning Journal*, the Yiddish daily newspaper, calling for a cantor to officiate for the coming High Holidays in Caldwell, New Jersey. The ad read that the job would pay $350.

I already had a job lined up to sing at a synagogue in Toledo, Ohio, that was going to pay me $1,600, quite an impressive amount in those days. Even though I already had this job, my brothers and I decided to go to Caldwell for the audition purely as a lark.

When we arrived at the synagogue, there was a full room of candidates already waiting in line. In fact, the line stretched out well into the street. Who knew so many Jewish men in New Jersey were part-time cantors? It was August, the heat was sweltering, and the synagogue had no air conditioning. It was unbearable inside.

They called in one candidate after another. Each gave his best version of an "aria" performance. The session went on for hours. Since we were in line to audition, my six brothers and I were called in one at a time. At one point, the president of the synagogue came out, sweating profusely.

"Who are these Schiffs?" he asked. "Are all seven of you related?"

We informed him that we were brothers.

"Look boys," he said. "It is terribly hot in there, so just send in your best."

My brother Joseph was really taken aback with this response.

"You advertised in the paper," he said angrily. "Therefore, you are obligated to hear each one of us."

We all forced the issue, to the great consternation of the search committee. After six of us had completed our auditions, the president came out to speak with Irving.

"Hey Mr. Schiff," he said, wiping sweat from his face with an enormous handkerchief. "Are you also going to audition?"

"No," my brother answered. "I'm the driver."

P.S. None of us got the job.

In 1950, a neighbor of mine moved to Atlanta and recommended me to a synagogue there as a cantor for the High Holidays. We signed a contract for $1,000. One day during the summer, I received a telephone call from a man who said he was a cantor in a neighboring synagogue in Atlanta. He invited me to visit him on Long Island, where he was visiting. Wishing to be a good neighbor, I accepted his invitation. During the course of the visit, he asked me to sing some cantoral prayers. I tried to avoid that because it was Tisha B'av, a fast day, and I'd had no food or water since the day before. I knew my singing would be compromised. He kept urging me to sing, and I finally relented.

A few days later, I received a letter from the president of the congregation I was to serve in a few weeks. The letter said that the cantor I sang for reported that I wasn't good enough to serve as their cantor. Therefore, he was canceling our contract. I asked my political science professor at Brooklyn College about this. He told me that a contract was a contract and that not having heard me in person does not minimize the sanctity of our agreement. He recommended a lawyer he knew to handle my case. The lawyer confirmed the validity of the contract. He proceeded to write to the president, holding him to the contract, and suggested that I immediately take steps to find a new position. The president sent me a check for $250 as a settlement. My attorney advised me to accept it and drop the case.

"Southern courts don't like to rule in favor of Yankees," he explained. "They can delay repeatedly, and you will have to keep going down to Atlanta." Since I lived in New York at the time, his suggestion seemed reasonable and I accepted the check and signed the release. In the meantime, I secured a job in a small congregation on Long Island for $350. All in all, it was a large drop from what I had received a year earlier in Toledo, Ohio.

However, I received my first significant lesson: Be cordial, but not trusting. I should never have sung in front of a competing cantor. (Then again, considering they are men of the cloth, should cantors really be undermining each other?) It was a costly lesson that remained with me for years.

As a young cantor in 1948

In 1954, I was hired to be the Cantor at Anshe Sholom Congregation in Chicago, the synagogue of my future wife and her family. That year, the New York Giants were playing the Cleveland Indians in the World Series. The Giants had beaten the Indians three games in a row. The fourth game was on Yom Kippur. Of course it was a day game in those years, before they added lights to the stadiums. Everyone in Chicago was rooting for the Indians, another midwestern city.

Right in the middle of the service, as I was chanting one of the more dramatic prayers of the day, the synagogue president approached the pulpit and whispered in my ear.

"Cantor, please pray harder. The Indians are losing."

I couldn't exactly interrupt the service, so I didn't respond. A short while later—maybe an inning had passed, I was guessing—the president came over to me again.

"Cantor, pray harder. It's the seventh inning and the Indians are still losing. If they lose today, it's all over."

Again, I couldn't respond. He shrugged and walked away. Soon after, just as I was completing the final prayers, he came back a third time.

"Cantor, I think your prayers are not very effective today. The Indians just lost."

Since I had completed the service I was finally permitted to talk.

"On the contrary," I said. "My prayers were very effective. I'm a Giants fan."

"You son of a gun," the president said, laughing heartily. "If we would have known that, we would never have hired you."

A week earlier, just after Rosh Hashanah, as I was preparing to return home to New York, my future wife's father asked me to do him a favor. He was a *shochet*, a ritual slaughterer of kosher cattle, in the Armour packinghouse company in Chicago. To perform his work, he used several huge, sharp knives, almost as large as a machete. He asked me to bring several of them to New York with me and take them to a knife-sharpening specialist in the Bronx. Since I was trying to get his consent to marry his daughter, I couldn't really say no.

I carried those long, sharp knives on the plane and brought them to the specialist. A few days later, I returned to Chicago, armed and ready to conduct Yom Kippur services and score points with my future father-in-law.

I often wonder what would happen if I attempted to take the knives on a plane today when the airlines won't even let me fly with a nail clipper. How tranquil and trusting those good old days were. The task of carrying the knives back and forth was a small price to pay for Shirley's hand.

As for spending the rest of my life as a cantor, I'm happy I became a rabbi, and Shirley is happy I still sing to her once in a while.

On one of my visits to Shirley's home, I asked her father for her hand.

"If you want my daughter," he said. "You must take all of her. I don't give handouts."

4
Shirley

IN 1952, I WAS HIRED to conduct the High Holiday services as cantor in South Bend, Indiana. After Rosh Hashanah, my host gave me $20 and suggested I visit Chicago, which I had never seen before.

On my first day in Chicago, I visited with Rabbi Isaac Small, a leading Orthodox rabbi in Chicago, who was the brother-in-law of Rabbi Moshe Feinstein, the head of the Mesifta Tifereth Jerusalem in New York, who ordained me as a rabbi two years later.

That evening, I had dinner with Rabbi Small and his wife. The next morning, I visited the Yeshiva where one of the students, Aryeh Rotman, who later became the rabbi of Beth Israel in Miami Beach, took me around and showed me the school.

I asked Aryeh if he knew any young ladies I could meet while I was in Chicago.

"I don't know any," he said. "But I'll ask my sister; she knows a lot of girls."

On the phone, she mentioned various girls, who Aryeh then described to me. One girl she mentioned sounded special but Aryeh said she wouldn't go with me.

As his sister completed her list, Aryeh asked, "Which one would you be interested in meeting?"

"How about the one who wouldn't go with me?" I asked. "Why won't she go with me? She doesn't even know me."

"Oh, she's a beautiful girl, Sol. On Shabbat, when she walks by the yeshiva, all the boys stare at her, admiring her good looks."

"That's the kind of girl I would like to meet," I said. "Could your sister give me her phone number?"

"You cannot just call her," Aryeh said. "You have to know someone who knows her who will make the introduction."

I said the only one I know in Chicago is Rabbi Isaac Small.

"Oh boy," Aryeh said, "He is her uncle."

I immediately called Rabbi Small to ask for his niece's phone number.

"Come over and we'll talk," he said, which I did, as soon as possible. Rabbi Small asked about my vocational plans and said that since I was a cantor, becoming a rabbi would put me in a good position. He later called Dora Miller, his sister, and they arranged to have me call her daughter, Shirley, the next day.

Finally, the next morning arrived and I called Shirley and introduced myself.

"I met Aryeh Rotman at the yeshiva," I began. "And he asked me if I had seen all the beautiful things in Chicago. Yes, I told him. I believe I have. 'Did you see Shirley Miller?' he asked. I said 'No,' to which he said, 'Then you haven't seen all the beautiful things in Chicago.'"

With that I asked Shirley for a date, which she accepted. On the date, she asked me where we were going. I said "In New York, when a date is so-so, you take her to a movie. When she is special, you take her to a play."

"So where are we going?" she asked.

"To a play," I said.

The story has a happy ending since we got married three years later.

The first joke I told Shirley on our first date went like this:

"Do you know how they got the name Staten Island?

"When Columbus was crossing the ocean, he was looking for dry land to settle on. As he looked into the distance, he seemed to see land and asked, ''S tat an Island?'"

I told that story many times.

One day, after I told it to some friends, our son, Jeffrey, who was about ten at the time, approached his mother.

"You married dad for that joke?" he asked.

"Of course," she replied. "He told other jokes that were worse."

While I was courting Shirley, her parents invited me for a Friday night meal. At the last minute, they had to leave home to attend a family funeral in Peoria, Illinois, so Shirley was left alone to prepare our dinner. Unbeknownst to me, Shirley had no cooking experience. In desperation, she asked her neighbor to help her with the menu. The neighbor recommended making chopped liver, which Shirley would make while her neighbor prepared the rest of the meal. Shirley thought that was a good choice. Liver should be easy. She broiled it, but unfortunately the liver got burnt. Instead of throwing it out, she ground it up and served it as the first course.

To her great surprise, instead of hearing me complain that the liver was burnt, Shirley heard me say, "My, it's the best liver I ever ate." She was extremely happy because her father always complained about his wife's cooking. She said to herself, "This is the man for me." This incident can be characterized as "De Libe Brent," which is Yiddish for "The Love Burns." In this case,

Libe (love) is a play on the word liver, or "The liver is burning." Evidently, this didn't hurt our relationship. Shirley and I got married and she became an excellent cook. Although she never burnt the liver again, the Libe (love) is still sizzling.

Shirley crowned as a beauty queen at Herzl Junior College in Chicago, 1953

Shirley and I, soon after we were engaged in 1954

At least one of us felt at home in the kitchen. Honestly, I was quite comfortable there when it only involved eating, but my culinary skills were another thing. You could say they were indescribable.

When Shirley once went to Chicago for the weekend to visit her parents, she prepared me some Shabbat food and left instructions on how to work the stove. (It is forbidden by Jewish law to use electrical appliances on Shabbat. However, timers are permitted). After Shabbat, when I spoke to Shirley on the phone, she asked me about the food. I said it was cold, that the stove had not turned on.

The next time Shirley went away, she left very detailed instructions on how to work the stove. After Shabbat, I called her.

"Did the fire go on in the stove?" she asked.

"Yes," I said.

"And how was the food?"

"Cold."

"Why?" she said, thoroughly confused.

"Well," I said sheepishly. "The instructions didn't say to put the food in the stove."

This is like the story of a newlywed who put a chicken in the stove and left to do some errands. When she returned, she opened the stove and saw the chicken curled up in the pot, saying, "Lady, put on the fire or give me a sweater. I'm freezing to death."

In 1978, Shirley and I were in San Francisco for a convention. We arranged a reunion with former members of our congregation in Dubuque, Iowa, who were now living in San Francisco.

As we reminisced, one of them said, "I'll never forget your wedding." (Our wedding had taken place in Chicago soon after I assumed the position in Iowa.) The one making the comment had never been to an Orthodox wedding before, and many of the procedures were novel to him.

"I remember after the dinner, all the men ran into the kitchen to see if the food was kosher," he explained.

Shirley and I stared at each other in puzzlement. Why would they check if the food was kosher? Those attending an Orthodox wedding usually assume the food is kosher and don't feel any need to inspect it. We smiled and continued our delightful evening. As we left, we discussed that strange comment and concluded the following: After the wedding dinner is over, the men usually gather at the head table for Sheva Brachot, a special prayer service. Our friend had probably asked someone where the men were going. I'm guessing someone was joking with our friend when they told him the men were going into the kitchen to see if the food was kosher. We wondered how many people he must have told this story to over the years.

Shirley and I once took a one-day cruise to Freeport in the Bahamas. We visited a casino, and at one point, we both went to the restroom. When I returned to the main room, I began talking to one of the gambling officials about certain aspects of the machines. After our conversation, I returned to the restroom area to find Shirley. When I didn't find her, I asked a security officer if they could page her. I was told they didn't do that.

I continued walking around, to no avail. An announcement was made that the last cab would be leaving in a few minutes to return to the ship. I had to decide quickly whether to leave or keep looking for Shirley, even though that meant I might miss the boat. I got into a taxi, and, as the driver was about to pull out, I saw Shirley come out of the casino looking very distraught. I quickly yelled to the driver to stop. Shirley and I were united at last and returned safely to the ship. But our perception of the event was very different from each other. I simply thought that after not finding me she would have left and we would meet up on board. Shirley's reasoning was that she would not leave without me and that she assumed I had remained to look for her.

The debate as to whether it was best to stay or go continues to this day.

Many years later, while Shirley and I were on a Jewish Federation mission to Israel, we had an adventure that has become somehow typical of our lives together.

We had arranged to visit my nephew and his family on a Saturday night after a gathering of our group at the Israel Museum in Jerusalem. We left early to keep our date. However, we couldn't find a taxi anywhere. The museum was located in an area that was essentially dormant over the weekend.

When I saw a police car down the road with its lights flashing I approached it with my best "nebbish" attitude, hoping to use that sense of charming helplessness to procure some much-needed assistance.

"My wife and I cannot find a taxi to take us to my family in Har Norf," I said to the police officer as he rolled down his window. "We feel lost and don't know what to do."

The officer told me he could drive us to a cabstand. I called to Shirley who was standing up the road, gesturing at me, trying to find out what was going on.

"Penny trouble!" I said to her, referencing the story of how I finagled a penny from that man back in Brooklyn when I was a young boy. By that point in our terrific marriage, it had become our code for acting clever in certain challenging situations. Shirley immediately got the message and began running quickly to join me in the police car.

As we were leaving the area, the police officer said, "Tonight is a quiet night with no calls for any crimes or emergencies, so I'll drive you to your destination."

As we drove through a shopping district, Shirley noticed reflections in the store windows of flashing red lights.

"I think we are being followed by a police car," she said to the police officer in the front seat. She soon realized that what she was seeing was us. Shirley whispered to me whether it would be appropriate to give the police officer a tip for his kind services.

"Hmm," I said. "Giving a tip to a police officer doesn't seem quite kosher."

Meanwhile, the police officer had difficulty locating the address and so we stopped a few times for directions. As we rolled through the neighborhood, people started poking their heads out of their front doors to see what was bringing out the police. We saw another nephew, Zev, who was to join us, walking with his family. We stopped the police car, got out, and thanked him profusely. Shirley was especially gracious and the policeman seemed smitten.

When we entered the apartment of our nephew, Avrom, who had seen the commotion developing on the street, we told him what happened.

"If there is anyone that can get a police escort, it's my Uncle Shlomie," he said.

"There's only one person in the whole world I could ever have an adventure with like this," I replied. "And that's my beautiful partner in crime, Shirley."

Someone once asked me, "How does your wife feel about being married to a famous man?"

I said, "One of her benefits is that I give her my autograph every night—at no cost."

"Yeah," Shirley remarked. "And I get to cash all the checks."

The truth is, I'm infinitely richer because I married Shirley Miller a long, long time ago. Smartest thing I've ever done.

The Miller Family, 1979

Shirley and I on our wedding day, February 6, 1955

Shirley won a beauty contest at Herzl Junior College in Chicago, which reminds me of a grandmother I once met who was wheeling her granddaughter down the street. Someone looked at the little one and said, "What a beautiful baby," to which the grandmother responded, "You should see her pictures."

I saw both Shirley and her pictures and I loved them both. After over a half century of marital bliss, I love them even more. The fact is, what brought us together pales to what keeps us together.

5

A Most Unlikely Pulpit

I N NOVEMBER 1954, soon after I got engaged to Shirley Miller in Chicago, I was looking for a job. I had just completed serving as cantor in Shirley's family synagogue for the High Holidays. Shirley's father, who had just lost his job as shochet (ritual slaughterer) at Armour and Company in Chicago, got a job in Dubuque, Iowa, where he became friendly with the townspeople. They asked him if he knew of a rabbi, since theirs had just resigned.

"Oy, do I have a rabbi for you," he said. He called me immediately and arranged for my audition. The main interrogator at the interview was Wolf Berk, the town's elder statesman. Among his questions were, "Rabbi, do you believe that a rabbi should send a bill to a member of the congregation, demanding a fee for services and immediate payment?"

It was obvious what answer he was looking for.

"Absolutely not," I said, with a firm tone.

He then asked, "Do you believe it is proper for a rabbi to walk his dog through downtown on Rosh Hashanah?"

I gave the obvious answer by again stating firmly, "Absolutely not."

Wolf Berk gave an affirmative nod to the committee, which immediately voted unanimously to accept me as its rabbi.

After the first service I conducted in my synagogue in Dubuque, Iowa, I walked to the rear of the synagogue to greet the congregants. Among the well wishers was an old lady who approached me with confidence.

"Rabbi, I loved your sermon," she said. "It was short but brief."

In December of 1954, my first (and very unexpected) rabbinic assignment took place at a B'nai B'rith meeting in the social hall of the synagogue. During the evening, someone came into the room and announced that Mrs.

Wolf Berk, the wife of our oldest and most revered community leader, had just had a heart attack. We were sitting at a long table. Everyone turned to the left as if asking, "What do we do?" When the last one turned to me, I likewise turned to my left, only to find I was at the end.

All the eyes were suddenly on me. I realized that I was their leader and needed to do something. I asked that the meeting be adjourned and that we move to the sanctuary for prayer. Without a prayer book or any sort of preparation, I began reciting. The trouble was that in saying the prayer by heart, I inadvertently began reciting an Amoleh—a prayer for the dead—instead of a Misheberach, a get-well prayer. When I finished, my father-in-law, who was visiting, uttered a few subtle words to me.

"The woman is still living; don't do that again."

I guess I didn't do too much harm. Mrs. Berk survived through the three and a half years I remained in Dubuque.

In February 1955, Shirley and I came to Miami Beach for our honeymoon. We had heard a lot about Rabbi Irving Lehrman of Temple Emanu-El. He enjoyed a reputation as a master sermonizer. At that time, I was the spiritual leader of Congregation Beth El in Dubuque, Iowa. Through a member of my congregation, Meyer

Zuckerman, who had a winter membership in Temple Emanu-El, I was able to obtain tickets for Friday night services.

When we arrived, there were mobs of people outside, trying to get in. It was like a rock concert. The service was magnificent and Rabbi Lehrman's sermon was awe-inspiring. After the service, he greeted us at the door. We introduced ourselves, and I asked some questions about preparing sermons.

Shirley and I spent the next hour walking along Collins Avenue, repeating what we remembered of the sermon. Since we couldn't write on the Sabbath, we felt that if we repeated it a few times, we could remember it and write it down afterward.

When we moved to Miami three and a half years later, Rabbi Lehrman and I became close colleagues. I told him how impressed we had been with his sermon and that we repeated it to each other following the service so that we could write it down after the Sabbath.

In 1989, the Rabbinical Association honored me on the occasion of my 25th anniversary as its executive vice president. We had a luncheon at Temple Emanu-El and I asked Rabbi Lehrman to be the main speaker. In his talk, Rabbi Lehrman recalled how we had come to his synagogue during our honeymoon.

"Rabbi Schiff told me later on, 'you know, Rabbi Lehrman, when we were in Miami for our honeymoon, your sermon was the highlight.'" Suddenly, I saw four hundred pairs of eyes staring at me. I made a gesture, which said in effect—not *the* highlight but *a* highlight.

It certainly wasn't the first time I had misspoken. I had years of experience. Back in Dubuque, I had once conducted a funeral for a man that was held on a Friday. I used as my text, "When the angels visit a Jewish home on Friday night and see the candles lit, they say, 'May next week be the same.'" The next Friday, I officiated at a funeral for another member of that family. I was hoping the family didn't feel that I had jinxed them. I always regretted the text I chose that first day.

By the time I was about to commemorate my first year in Dubuque, I found out that my reputation was building. After a service celebrating this milestone, a man approached me.

"Rabbi," he said. "We didn't know what sin was until you came to town."

I once gave a speech at a fundraising function. The chairman introduced me in the following way.

"I envy our guest speaker because his name is Solomon, and the biblical Solomon had a thousand wives."

When I got up to speak, I said, "There is no reason to be envious of the biblical Solomon. If Solomon had a thousand wives, he also had a thousand mothers-in-law."

6
Mitzvahs in Miami

SHIRLEY AND I ENCOUNTERED blatant racism for the first time when we visited Miami on our honeymoon in 1955. We boarded a local city bus and noticed black passengers standing in the back while empty seats were available in the front.

"There are many empty seats in the front," we said to the folks in the back. "Why don't you sit down there?"

They laughed. The bus driver called us over.

"Where are you from?" he asked, as if we had stepped into the Twilight Zone.

"I am from New York and my wife is from Chicago," I replied.

"You are now in the South," the driver responded. "Blacks down here don't sit in the front of the bus."

In 1958, sixteen years after first learning about the Holocaust while standing in front of Madison Square Garden with my father, my promise to him was realized when I became the rabbi of Congregation Beth El in Miami. This orthodox synagogue had recently become the spiritual home of the New Americans Social Club, whose members were Holocaust survivors.

I became their rabbi and mentor, as most of them had no families when they survived—only each other. I had many occasions to counsel them, share their pain, officiate at their funerals, and participate in their Yom Hashoah observances, as well as their weddings, Bar Mitzvahs, and other occasions. Of all my activities since becoming a rabbi in 1954, my service to the Holocaust survivor community is the one I cherish most, since it comes closest to satisfying the promise I made all those years ago.

My father, of blessed memory, lived in the United States for about fifty years. He spoke very little English, associating mostly with his Yiddish-speaking friends and associates. When we moved to Miami, I corresponded with him in Yiddish.

I wrote him that I was elected secretary of the Rabbinical Association of Greater Miami.

"My son," he wrote back. "I am proud of your accomplishment, but tell me, with all the rabbis in Miami, they couldn't find a rabbi to be secretary who has a better handwriting than you?"

My father had beautiful handwriting. He was the scribe to one of the great European rabbis who relied on my father to make the words of the manuscript attractive and easy to read.

For years, the Rabbinical Association of Greater Miami urged the Greater Miami Jewish Federation to establish a chaplaincy program. The federation thought this was a religious venture that should be handled by the rabbis. The rabbis argued that they had all they could handle, attending to the needs of their members. Also, an overwhelming number of Jews in the Miami area were unaffiliated; and with this being a tourist community, there was no rabbi responsible for them when they found themselves in hospitals or other institutions.

Two things helped convince the federation to finally agree. First, our association planned a public installation of officers at Temple Beth Sholom on Miami Beach. We invited Rabbi Harold Gordon, the executive vice president of the New York Board of Rabbis, to be the guest speaker. We also invited some of the federation leaders. Rabbi Gordon stressed the importance of a chaplaincy program, sponsored by the federation. He gave the same message the following day at a joint meeting. The federation was impressed with his arguments and immediately appointed a study commission to consider the matter. The second incident occurred on a cruise ship, the *Yarmouth Castle,* which set sail from Miami early in 1966. A fire broke out, resulting in close to one hundred fatalities through drowning and smoke inhalation. Many of the injured survivors were brought to our Miami hospitals. As the rabbi at Congregation Beth El, the closest shul to Jackson Memorial Hospital where most of the patients were brought, I was called in to minister to these victims and their families.

I asked the Chaplains Office to save the admission cards of Jewish passengers and keep them for a month. They collected sixty cards. Our association arranged a meeting between our past presidents and the federation leadership. Each of the rabbis spoke for the establishment of a chaplaincy program.

In my remarks, I told of some moving experiences with patients I visited, including an old man who tried to kill himself with an overdose the day before Yom Kippur. He was extremely remorseful and had asked for a rabbi. I told several other stories of touching cases I had encountered. I described my experience with the victims of the *Yarmouth Castle.*

I then placed sixty cards on the table.

"Who is responsible for these patients?" I asked.

As the meeting ended, we left the committee to discuss the matter. That night, while attending a dinner at a local congregation, Harold Thurman, a member of the committee, approached me with good news.

"Mazel Tov, Sol," he said. "You have your chaplaincy." The two stipulations were that I was to be the part-time director and that the program would be evaluated after six months. Sam Heiman, a past president of the federation who served as the chairman of the study commission, became the first chairman of the Community Chaplaincy Service. My employment began on May 16, 1966, and six months later the commission recommended that my position be made permanent.

On Friday, May 31, 1963, an interfaith meeting was held at the Columbus Hotel. The meeting brought together clergy representing Miami's major religious denominations. A joint statement was issued, stating, "We proclaim that racial prejudice, discrimination, and segregation are a violation of justice, and an affront to the dignity of man." The statement called on "all citizens of our community to recognize the importance and urgency of arriving at discussions which could solve racial problems."

At an Israel Bonds dinner in Miami during the 1960s

Bishop Coleman F. Carroll, head of the Catholic Diocese of Miami, read the statement to the press. As the president of the Rabbinical Association of Greater Miami, I was also invited to participate. At that time, calling for the elimination of racial prejudice, discrimination, and segregation was extremely bold and challenging. All three were widespread in our community, with separate restrooms marked Female White, Female Black and Male White, Male Black, as well as public water fountains marked White and Black.

On June 11, 1963, only a few days after that historic proclamation on equal rights, the Community Relations Board of the Miami–Dade County was formed to address these issues of discrimination. Now, close to fifty years after its establishment, the Community Relations Board (CRB) can look back with pride at its great accomplishments in helping to reverse the terrible consequences of discrimination.

The CRB has been in the forefront of bringing calm to situations of extreme stress and pain. For example, in 1980, one of the worst racial riots in the United States took place in Miami, triggered by an all-white jury exonerating a group of white police officers in the killing of a black motorcyclist, Arthur McDuffie. During the ensuing riot, fifteen people were killed and close to two hundred injured. It was the CRB members and staff, including myself as president, who were on the streets, trying to calm the people's anger.

A similar event occurred in January 1989, when a white police officer named William Lozano shot and killed two black motorcyclists. During the ensuing riots, which lasted for three days, the CRB was there on the streets to help diffuse much of the anger and bitterness. One of the lessons we learned from the earlier McDuffie riot was that there was no television coverage of the trial. This led to many rumors, speculations, and misunderstandings about the trial, with many feeling that the trial was unfair.

In the subsequent trial of Lozano, the CRB, in addition to patrolling the streets, arranged for a court television channel to cover the entire trial. One of our CRB attorneys at the time, Don Bierman, who would later serve as its chairman, aired a special program every night, explaining all the steps that had taken place during that day's session. In this way, everyone concerned about the trial was able to view it along with various explanations and interpretations. As a result, there were no ambiguities or misconceptions, which helped to prevent the pitfalls of the previous trial and enabled everyone to see that the trial was fair. Because of that, the riots were far less fiery and hateful, with no deaths and hardly any injuries reported.

With President George H. Bush, Sr., 1990

Another example of CRB's good work occurred on June 28, 1990, when Nelson Mandela came to Miami to speak about his anti-apartheid campaign. There was much anger among Miami's Cuban community for Mandela's refusal to disavow Fidel Castro. Many Cuban mayors of Miami–Dade County, including Miami's Mayor Suarez, issued a statement condemning Mandela. The members of the black community were equally upset by this insult to Mandela.

A vociferous demonstration by both sides in front of Miami Beach's Convention Hall (where Mandela was to speak) threatened to become an uncontrollable riot. Again, the CRB was there, meeting with both sides and helping to calm the waters, resulting in no deaths and no injuries.

Rather than exhorting protesters to violence, leaders of the black community, led by a well-known black attorney named H.T. Smith, called for a boycott, by which no black convention would come to the Miami area. This boycott lasted several years until reconciliation was arranged, and the boycott was called off, welcoming in the construction of a black-owned hotel on Miami Beach.

During the Cold War in the early 1960s, as the United States shadowboxed with the Soviet Union, civil defense preparations kicked into high gear. People were building air-raid shelters and stocking them with food and a host of supplies. Dade County's Sheriff Kelly organized a Civil Defense Chaplains Emergency Corps, consisting of a hundred volunteer clergy of all faiths who would minister to the spiritual needs of the people in the case of most any disaster. In October 1965, I was elected as the group's president. One of the benefits of serving in this corps was that in an air raid (in those days, we feared Soviet atomic bomb attacks) we were authorized to be out on the street in order to help with the disaster. We were given helmets with the letters "CD" on them. We were also given material from the National Civil Defense

Department. In a list of instructions on what to do in case an atomic bomb fell, the first one was "be calm." When I told Shirley of my duties as a CD chaplain, she was not very impressed with my paraphernalia or the accompanying perk of being out on the street during an atomic disaster.

"During a disaster," she said quite assuredly, "your place is to be home with me and the children." Thankfully, our services were never required.

As a rabbi, especially one with an ongoing, dedicated congregation, the responsibilities are many, and even though I had a very thorough education and the best of training, nothing could have prepared me for some of the situations I have faced as a rabbi, especially in the early days in Dubuque, Iowa. And even as I gathered experience, I still faced many puzzling predicaments.

One day, I went to see a congregant who was a patient at Mount Sinai Medical Center. He had already seen several visitors. As I was about to leave, his wife wanted to give me a contribution. I am generally reluctant to take money for visits but I couldn't dissuade her.

"If you want to make a contribution," I said, "please write a check to the Greater Miami Jewish Federation."

She began searching for cash. As she was looking, her checkbook kept popping up in her purse.

"Write a check," her husband blurted out.

The woman kept rummaging through her bag for cash. After several more suggestions that she write a check, her husband pleaded, "Why don't you just give him a check?"

"Your surgery is Thursday," she said matter-of-factly. "The check will never clear by then."

"But if the surgery fails," he replied, "you can always stop the check."

The man's wife immediately wrote out a generous check and I had no choice by that time but to accept it. It was a lucky day for one of my preferred charities.

A rabbi never knows who might wander into his syna-gogue office on any given day. A woman visited me once to say she had Yahrzeit (anniversary memorial) for her father. She asked if she could observe the Yahrzeit in Miami even though he is buried in Jacksonville.

"Of course," I said. "We have a reciprocal agree-ment with Jacksonville. They recognize our Yahrzeits and we recognize theirs." I'm not sure if she was amused but she did show up for minyan.

Another time, a woman visited me in my office and asked me to make a Misheberach (a prayer for the sick) for some of her relatives. She gave me the names of each person and told me their sickness. Then she told me that she had another sick cousin. I waited for the name but she didn't say a word.

"Do you want me to say a prayer for him?" I asked.

"No," she said. "He has arthritis and there is no cure for that."

She seemed to imply that before G-d heals someone, He looks into the medical journal to see whether or not there is a cure for that illness.

I was making rounds at the Cedars of Lebanon Hospital when I was paged to the nurse's station for an emergency telephone call.

A woman's voice said, "Rabbi, I have a big problem. My husband, Maxwell, didn't get up this morning and I'm afraid he might be dead."

"Maybe he's just sleeping late," I replied, obviously without thinking.

"No," she said quite assuredly. "He never sleeps this late. He gets up at 8 a.m. and I give him his coffee. He likes it hot and it's 9:30 already and he hasn't gotten up and the coffee is getting cold."

"Did you try waking him?" I asked delicately.

"No," she replied right away. "He might be asleep."

"Did you call a doctor?" I asked, wondering where this conversation was going.

"What for, Rabbi? If he's asleep, he doesn't need a doctor. If he's dead, a doctor wouldn't help, either."

I was going to tell her, "At least you'll have someone to drink the coffee," but instead I said, "Did you try to feel his pulse?"

"No," she answered matter-of-factly. "He wakes very easily, and he'll be grouchy all day if I wake him up."

"Did you try putting your finger to his nose to see if he's breathing?"

"No, he's very ticklish," she said. "I feel terrible because when he wakes up, the coffee will be cold and he hates cold coffee."

I couldn't understand what her main concern was, her husband or the coffee. Running out of ideas, I suggested he be given a brain scan.

"What do his brains got to do with whether he's dead or alive?" she asked. "Too bright Maxwell never was, although he always knew the difference between hot and cold coffee. Besides, he may be dead and you're talking about giving him an I.Q. test?"

I was stumped.

"Maybe you could see which is getting colder faster," I offered. "The coffee or your husband."

"My husband has never been as hot as the coffee. It's an unfair test."

She left the phone for a few moments and returned, saying quite plainly, "I believe he's dead." I had no idea how she had determined this. Maybe she gave him the coffee test and he failed. Someone listening to the conversation remarked, "It's the first time a rabbi was asked to pronounce someone dead over the phone."

"Now that he is dead," she interrupted, "what should I do?"

"Call a funeral home to arrange for his burial," I told her.

"Do I need a funeral home?" she asked. "Can't I just take him to the cemetery?"

"If you don't mind my asking," I began. "How are you going to get him to the cemetery? By taxi?"

I proceeded to help her make the funeral arrangements and worked with her through her initial grief process. A year later, as we came to the cemetery to unveil her husband's tombstone, I read what may be the most unusual inscription I have ever seen on a tombstone:

Here lies Maxwell – good to the last drop.

A newspaper reporter from the Gannett media company once called our home, informing me that according to the Florida State Marriage Regulations, all weddings performed by rabbis in the last one hundred years are not legal. The reason is the wording in the Florida regulations, which list religious representatives authorized to perform marriages as "Ministers of the Gospel." Since Jews do not believe in the Gospel, they are therefore technically excluded from performing marriages.

I brought this flaw to the attention of our state legislators, who asked me what term would include religious representatives of all religious denominations.

"Clergy," I suggested.

This term was entered into law, which made weddings performed by rabbis officially kosher. Since this was only a technical matter, the law would not retroactively overturn marriages previously performed by rabbis. Oh well, another day, another skirmish with the red tape of state politics.

You might think being a rabbi, and if I say so myself, one who was becoming a little bit well known around town, might offer some special privileges when it came to law and order. But I found out soon enough that this was not exactly the case, at least not in Miami.

One time while driving, I made a left turn from the left lane on U.S. Route 1 onto Red Road, in South Miami. A police motorcyclist pulled me over and gave me a ticket, claiming I had turned after the arrow turned red, blocking oncoming traffic, including him.

While I waited to appear in traffic court, I heard the following case of a young man:

"How do you plead?" asked the judge.

"It was not me," the young man said.

He explained that he was at work at the time of the violation, that he had punched in his time card at 9 a.m. and punched out at 5 p.m. and the citation time was listed as 11 a.m.

"Let's set a trial date," said the judge, "and bring witnesses to back your claim."

"How many witnesses should I bring?" the young man asked.

The judge said, "Young man, let me tell you something. My law professor in college used to tell us that it is possible to have a hundred clergy—rabbis, priests, and ministers—testifying one way, and one good witness testifying the opposite, and it is possible to believe that one witness over one hundred men of the cloth." (Implying that it was not the numbers but the quality of the witnesses that counts.)

"Solomon Schiff."

I heard my name announced as if it was shot out of a cannon. The judge didn't know that I was a rabbi.

Blood rushed to my head. I figured if I handled this right I should have an easy time.

I approached the judge, who asked me, "What is your name?"

"Your Honor," I began with a shaky confidence, "I am one of the one hundred clergymen that your law professor said you can never believe, no matter what they say. I am a rabbi."

The judge, who obviously felt a little embarrassed, burst into a hearty laugh.

"Get out of my court!" he bellowed. "Case dismissed."

Perfect timing!

Some of my community activities included serving as executive vice president of the Rabbinical Association of Greater Miami, an organization comprising one hundred rabbis from Orthodox, Conservative, Reform, and Reconstructionist synagogues. I held this position from 1964 until 2006, making me the longest-serving executive of any board of rabbis. I also served as director of chaplaincy for the Greater Miami Jewish Federation from 1966 to 2006.

Serving in this position often put me in contact with local, regional, and sometimes national media, as they sought the opinion of various clergy, depending on the nature of the news event.

In 1981, Israeli troops crossed into Lebanon to rout out the PLO, which had been terrorizing innocent Israeli citizens. They advanced quite rapidly until they came to Beirut, the capital, where they got bogged down for several weeks. Because the terrorists were holed up in various private dwellings, there was no way that Israeli forces could prevent civilian casualties.

Subsequently, I received a phone call from someone who identified himself as a staff person for CBS News. He said that he would like to interview a rabbi on the Israeli shelling of "innocent people." He asked if I thought it was right to shoot at civilians. I answered that it was terrible, but that the Israelis had an obligation to destroy the terrorists, and that by surrounding themselves with innocent people the PLO was also responsible for these innocent victims. All his questions were in a similar vein, questioning the morality of this action. He ended the interview by saying, "We will call you if we decide to use the interview."

That evening, I turned on the television and heard the announcer say, "When we return, we will hear about how American Jews are outraged at Israelis killing innocent people."

As the segment began, it showed a rabbi dressed in a *talit* (prayer shawl), speaking to his congregation. He said it was terrible how Israelis are taking innocent lives, how immoral it was, and that there was no justification for it. My impression was that CBS, determined to do a story criticizing Israel's actions, must have called enough rabbis until they got the opinion they sought. The venue of the interview was also questionable. There is virtually no service on a Wednesday night in which a rabbi is dressed in a *talit,* preaching to a congregation. The announcer did not say that this was one of the reactions of American Jews, or that there were a variety of views. Instead, he stated that this was the reaction of American Jews, implying that this view was unanimous. If this is not managing the news, I don't know what is.

Yitzchak Rabin served as prime minister of Israel on two different occasions. In 1978, between his two administrations, he spoke at the University of Miami's Hillel Foundation. I was asked to escort him in a limousine during his visit. Shirley and I wanted very much to have him in our home for dinner. We assumed that as a world figure, he would have many invitations for dinner.

When I picked him up at the airport, I showed him the itinerary for the day, and as he read the schedule I held my breath as he was coming to the dinner plans.

As he read "dinner at the Schiffs," he said, "Why should your wife bother?" I said it would be our honor.

I quickly called Shirley to inform her that Mr. Rabin would be coming. Before dinner, Shirley brought out some of our favorite Israeli liquors and offered them to him, which he declined. During dinner, Shirley again offered him the same drinks, which he again declined.

"Would you like some hard stuff?" she asked.

"What do you have?" Rabin replied.

"Scotch," Shirley said, hoping she had hit on something.

Mr. Rabin proceeded to have a couple of shots. Evidently, it wasn't that he didn't drink; it was merely a question of his choice of drinks.

After dinner, Mr. Rabin and I drove to the University of Miami. He checked into a nearby hotel and went up to his room to prepare for the lecture. While I waited in the lobby, I heard the university security guards discussing plans to take the prime minister to the campus. The security guard, who was driving a small yellow Volkswagen, explained what would be happening.

"The rabbi will ride in the limousine, as a decoy, and we will take the prime minister in our Volkswagen."

Wait a minute, I thought; I came along for the ride but not to risk my life. We followed their plan and fortunately travel to the campus was uneventful. We passed a heavy cadre of shouting demonstrators, but no harm was done.

During our dinner, we took a lot of pictures as a keepsake of that important family event. Unfortunately, none of the pictures came out, since for the first and only time, I didn't thread the film properly. A few months later, I happened to see Mr. Rabin at a local function. I told him how disappointed I was that the pictures hadn't come out.

He said in a very reassuring voice, "Don't worry. I will visit you again and you will have a chance to get your pictures." Of course, that prediction never took place. A few years later, in 1995, after leaving the platform at a peace rally in Tel Aviv, Prime Minister Rabin was fatally shot in the back by a gunman. The security issue, which seemed relatively unimportant at the time of his Miami visit, ended up being critical at the Tel Aviv rally. The lesson of this is tragic but obvious.

David Ben Gurion, the first prime minister of Israel, was a guest of a State of Israel Bonds national dinner at the Fontainebleau Hotel. Three rabbis representing the three streams of Judaism were asked to go up to his suite to escort him and his wife, Paula, down to the dinner.

The rabbis were Rabbi Irving Lehrman (Conservative), Rabbi Joseph Narot (Reform), and myself as the Orthodox one of the group. I was the only rabbi wearing a yarmulke.

With Israeli Prime Minister Yitzchak Rabin in Miami Beach, 1990

As we came into their suite, an aide introduced us to the prime minister.

"Zeh Rav Narot," meaning, "This is Rabbi Narot," to which Paula remarked, "Zeh Rav?"—"This is a rabbi?"

The aide then said, "Zeh Rav Lehrman," meaning, "This is Rabbi Lehrman," to which Paula remarked, "Zeh Rav?"—"This is a rabbi?"

He then introduced me, saying "Zeh Rav Schiff," meaning, "This is Rabbi Schiff," to which Ben Gurion remarked, "Zeh Rav!"—"This is a rabbi!"

Although not an orthodox Jew, Ben Gurion, nevertheless, looked at an orthodox rabbi as the one who most clearly and authentically represents Judaism. I'm not sure how my colleagues felt at that moment but I was very proud.

In 1986, I received a letter from Archbishop Edward McCarthy, the leader of the Archdiocese of Miami, marked "Personal and Confidential," informing me that Pope John Paul II was coming to Miami and would like to meet with the Jewish leadership of the United States while he was there. The purpose of his letter was to ask me how the Jewish community would regard such a visit. Would we welcome it? He needed to know so that plans could proceed for the meeting.

I discussed it with several Jewish leaders who gave a very positive response. I learned from the archbishop that the reason Miami was chosen for this meeting was that the archbishop had told the pope on several occasions about the warm and close relationship that exists

Israeli Prime Minister Golda Meir in 1971 at a State of Israel
Bonds dinner at the Fontainebleau Hotel in Miami Beach

in Miami between the Catholic and Jewish communities. Among these was a multifaith mission to Israel that he and I participated in and interfaith dialogue committees that we have had for many years.

We set up a committee to plan the event. The site chosen for the meeting was the Miami Art Museum. We had to devise a plan for allocating the limited number of seats. Our local Jewish community members were jockeying for seats with national Jewish organizations. They wanted to have all but a few of the 150 or so seats.

They were peeved to begin with that the meeting was not being held in New York, which they considered the capital of the Jewish world. Since the allocation procedure was delegated to Miami's Catholic leadership, and since we had a close relationship with them, we asked for a sizable number of seats for the local Jewish community.

During that summer, a crisis developed, which threatened to cancel the papal meeting. The pope had a meeting with Kurt Waldheim, formerly the secretary general of the United Nations, who had been exposed as a former Nazi officer. Since becoming the president of Austria, no nation had extended an invitation to him for an official visit. The Vatican was the first. On three different occasions that summer, I was invited to attend special Jewish leadership meetings in New York to discuss the crisis and whether or not we should cancel the papal meeting. My position was that we should continue to meet, since canceling would be offensive to the pope and set back whatever progress we had made in Catholic–Jewish relations. If we met with him, we could express our views on this and other issues. This position finally prevailed.

The papal meeting was under the umbrella of the Synagogue Council of America, comprised of six organizations: the rabbinic and the synagogue organizations

THE ARCHDIOCESE OF MIAMI
FROM THE RISING TO THE SETTING OF THE SUN IS THE NAME OF THE LORD TO BE PRAISED

OFFICE OF THE ARCHBISHOP

April 7, 1986

PERSONAL--CONFIDENTIAL

Rabbi Solomon Schiff
Rabbinical Association of Greater Miami
4200 Biscayne Boulevard
Miami, Florida 33137-0100

Dear Rabbi Schiff:

We have learned that on the occasion of the proposed visit of
Pope John Paul II to the United States in September of 1987,
His Holiness would like to have a brief good will visit with
representatives of the Jewish community and that Miami has been
proposed as the most appropriate place for such a visit.

At this very early stage, a suggestion has been made that we
explore the possibility of the Pope actually visiting a
synagogue. We have learned that the Holy Father plans a visit
to a synagogue in Rome within a few weeks.

Would you be able to tell me how such a proposal would be
received by Jewish leadership in Miami and, if there is a
positive reaction, which synagogue or temple would be proposed
for such a visit. Actually, at this stage, we are not certain
whether the visit to a synagogue or temple can be worked out
since his schedule will be very tight. It seems that whenever
the Pope moves he must be accompanied by a large entourage
which makes any visit to an additional site greatly time
consuming. It could be that we would invite representatives
of the Jewish community to meet him somewhere where he is
already scheduled to be, such as at my home where he will spend
the night or at the Cathedral where he will have a brief prayer
service upon his arrival, or at the place where he will address
priests of the United States.

I must ask that, at this moment, the plans not be made public.
However, I will be grateful for your reaction and advice.

Sincerely yours,

Edward A. McCarthy
Archbishop of Miami

EAM:mm
cc: The Reverend Robert N. Lynch

of the three major Jewish religious streams. According to the council's bylaws, any one of the constituent organizations could veto the actions of the council. The Rabbinical Council of America (RCA) wanted to veto the papal visit. Instead, they abstained from voting and the meeting was saved. Its only stipulation was that Rabbi Gilbert Klaperman, an RCA member who was to deliver the message on behalf of the Jewish leadership, would not be the one to address the pope at the meeting.

As the liaison between the Jewish and Catholic communities, I had quite a bit of public exposure during

Meeting Pope John Paul II in Miami, 1987

this period, with many TV and print media interviews. Two nights before the September 11, 1987, papal meeting, my wife, Shirley, and I were startled when we heard a commotion outside our house. A number of TV cameras with lights were aimed at our front door. Some Jewish militants had called the TV stations, informing them that they were going to picket me and create a confrontation. They barked out slogans and paraded signs, saying, "Rabbi Schiff, remember the six million Jews who were murdered in the Holocaust." And "Rabbi Schiff, the Pope didn't recognize Israel!" and other offensive slogans. Of course, we didn't open the door.

All of us who were to attend the papal meeting shared in a dinner the night before at the Omni Hotel, joined by Catholic and Jewish leaders. Nearly all of the cardinals of the United States were in attendance. We were all housed that night at the hotel. The next morning, we were taken to the meeting in buses, with a police escort.

At the meeting, the pope and our representative, Rabbi Mordecai Waxman, gave speeches. The pope lauded the Jewish people, referring to us their elder brothers, and recognized for our contributions to their faith. He lauded Israel as a home to many survivors.

We made several requests of the pope: to recognize Israel, to issue a strong denunciation of anti-Semitism, and to recognize that the Catholic community didn't do enough to save the Jews during the Holocaust. In the ensuing years, the pope responded with positive action on all three of these requests.

In the early 1990s, the pope finally gave official recognition to the State of Israel. In 2000, he made an extensive visit to Israel, placing a note in the Western Wall, asking forgiveness for the pain Christians inflicted on Jews throughout the ages. He condemned anti-Semitism, declaring it a sin. He used the Hebrew words *teshuvah* (repentance) and *Shoah* (the Holocaust), which reflected his sensitivity to the Jewish people. The teshuvah was for acts of anti-Semitism by Christians, leading

JOHN PAUL II

*A*RCHBISHOP EDWARD A. McCARTHY GIVES THANKS TO GOD FOR THE PRESENCE OF THE UNIVERSAL PASTOR AMONG THE PEOPLE OF SOUTH FLORIDA AND FOR THE SPIRITUAL RENEWAL ACCOMPLISHED BY HIS VISIT. HE WISHES TO EXPRESS HIS SINCERE GRATITUDE FOR YOUR PERSONAL CONTRIBUTION TO THIS HISTORIC VISIT WHICH WOULD NOT HAVE BEEN POSSIBLE WITHOUT YOUR DEDICATION. WITH A FERVENT PRAYER THAT WE WILL COMMIT OURSELVES IN A RENEWED ZEAL TO THE ESTABLISHMENT OF THE KINGDOM OF FAITH, PRAYER, AND LOVE, THESE GREETINGS ARE COMMENDED.

PRESENTED TO:
Rabbi Solomon Schiff

SEPTEMBER 1987   MIAMI, FLORIDA

A special recognition from the Pope, 1987

to the Shoah. The meeting was very meaningful and has had lasting effects in the process of reconciliation between Catholics and Jews.

Miami, because of its warm weather, attracts many homeless people. During the tourist season, when there are special events scheduled, such as the Super Bowl, the Orange Bowl, and the Pro Bowl, in order to prevent an embarrassment for the city the police would do a sweep and put many of the homeless in prison. In 1992, a lawsuit was filed against this practice. Judge Clyde Atkins, a federal judge, ruled that being homeless is not a crime, and therefore the homeless cannot be incarcerated. As a result of this ruling, Florida Governor Lawton Chiles formed a task force to study the problem of homelessness and recommend a solution. The chairman of the task force was a prominent community leader, Alvah Chapman. I was invited to be a member of the committee.

After meetings and research, we recommended that a one percent sales tax be added to all restaurant food and beverage bills in the county. The tax was approved in 1993. In May 1994, the Miami–Dade Homeless Trust was formed. I have been serving on the trust on and off since its establishment, including serving as its vice chairman. Miami–Dade County was the only community at the time that voted to tax itself for the benefit of the homeless.

The first year, the tax raised approximately seven million dollars. This amount was increased considerably over the next sixteen years. In addition, a homeless partnership organization was established. This is a nonprofit and a nongovernmental body that raises several million dollars a year. An annual allocation from the federal government is also added to the fund. Together, these funds have helped construct two Homeless Assistance Centers, one in Miami and the other in Homestead, Florida. Each center houses some five hundred individuals, who reside there for up to sixty days. The homeless are provided with a full range of services, including food and board, medical services, addiction treatment, vocational training, and early childhood education.

When the program started in 1994, there were approximately eight thousand homeless on the streets, with no residence and no services. With this new program, the number of homeless is down to fewer than eight hundred. After these residents complete their time at the centers, they are placed in intermediate and long-term facilities, with additional services offered.

In the Biblical story, when Cain killed his brother Abel, G-d asked him, "Where is Abel your brother?" To which Cain replied, "Am I my brother's keeper?" (Genesis 4:9)

Our community responded affirmatively:

"We are our brother's keeper."

We have responded in action, as well as in words, with a commitment to care for our brothers and sisters, pledging that their well-being is our obligation, and that their safety is our concern. Rather than use the expression, "Live and let live," I prefer a more active version, "Live and help live." Hopefully, this moral position will spread to other communities, so that all of G-d's children will be able to enjoy life to its fullest with security and justice for all. After all, we should be concerned for the last, the least, the lost, and the lonely.

And none of this is about being Jewish, Catholic, Buddhist, or anything else.

In February 2003, the National Conference of Community and Justice (NCCJ) presented me with a Distinguished Community Leadership Award. Among the other honorees was Alonzo Mourning, the star basketball player for the Miami Heat. When we posed for a group picture, I tried to stand away from Mr. Mourning, who looks twelve feet tall compared to me. He put his arm around my shoulders, indicating he wanted me to stand next to him.

"Nothing personal," I said to him, "but the reason I don't want to stand next to you is that you make me look shorter that I am."

"That's exactly why I want to stand next to you," Alonzo replied. "You make me look taller than I am." He won, and we were both right. That, as they say, is the long and short of it.

During the civil rights marches in the 1960s, many of those in the forefront of the marches were rabbis, including myself. During these marches, we wore traditional black yarmulkes, as is our religious custom. As time passed, the African American leaders of the marches linked our skullcaps with their struggle for freedom. They began to refer to them as "freedom caps." Many wanted to wear them when they marched. When they tracked down a yarmulke factory in New York, they ordered many dozens of black freedom caps. At first, the owner didn't know what freedom caps were. As the caller described it, the owner said, "Oh, freedom caps! Yes, we have a lot of them."

Very soon, the yarmulke manufacturer expanded his operation by adding sewing machines, workers, and materials. While trying to increase his business even more, he tried to entice his customers into purchasing white freedom caps. Not only were there no takers; once the civil rights marches began to slow down, the whole idea of freedom caps came to an end.

While the freedom cap business didn't last long, Jewish participation in the civil rights struggle went a long way in helping to bring the black community closer to its goal of freedom. One of the biggest results was the passage of the Civil Rights Act of 1965, which led to a series of equal rights opportunities. Now look where it's led: to the election of Barack Obama as president.

As I reflect on the ramifications of the civil rights movement, I see the monumental reversal of what Shirley and I experienced on that bus when we first arrived in Miami.

The first time I visited our Miami Archbishop, John C. Favalora in his office, I told him the story about when Abraham Joshua Heschel, the well-known rabbi, first visited Cardinal Francis Spellman. Heschel said, "How unusual is this? Here I am, wearing a black yarmulke, while you are wearing a red yarmulke. But we are always in the red and you are always in the black."

To which Spellman responded, "How I wish that were true."

And that was the beginning of a beautiful friendship.

7

How I Came to Pray for the Dolphins

In 1965, when the American Football League granted the city of Miami the opportunity to form a franchise, the local owners staged a contest to choose the name of the team. Our son, Elliot, submitted the name "Dolphins." Since there were so many others who submitted the same name they held a runoff to select the winning entry. The "chosen one" would be determined by guessing the closest score at the next Orange Bowl game. Elliot didn't win, but as a consolation prize, he received two complimentary tickets for the opening game of Miami's very first season. Unfortunately, the game was scheduled on a Friday night and we couldn't attend.

Soon afterward, we met the team's owner, Joe Robbie. In 1970, when the Dolphins became part of the venerable National Football League, he invited me to give a prayer before their last home game of the season, which we won, enabling us to advance to the playoffs for the first time in franchise history. This began a relationship I have enjoyed with the Robbie family and the Dolphins for well over thirty years. Joe and Elizabeth Robbie were guests for dinner in our home and I interviewed Joe several times on television programs sponsored by the Rabbinical Association of Greater Miami. A nicer man I've never met.

One season, after delivering another invocation at a Dolphins game, the team lost a real heartbreaker. Normally, after a game in which I gave the prayer, our custom was to join Joe Robbie and many sports figures and broadcasters for a victory celebration in a special reception room in the stadium.

On that day, feeling the sting of defeat, our son, Jeffrey asked if we were still going to go meet everyone. I said that I didn't think that Mr. Robbie would appreciate a visit at that time, so we had better skip it.

"Dad, if there is ever a time when Mr. Robbie needs a friendly face," Jeffrey responded, "it would be now." I took his advice and we went. The only two people in the reception room were Joe Robbie and Howard Cossel, the legendary sportscaster. Joe was in a down mood, but he told us how much he appreciated our visit. I told Jeffrey how smart I thought he was.

With Joe Robbie, original owner of the
Miami Dolphins football team, in 1971

During the first week of September 1972, only weeks after the massacre of eleven Israeli athletes at the Olympic Games in Munich, Germany, we held a special meeting at the Greater Miami Jewish Federation to discuss mobilizing public opinion against the terrorists.

Someone suggested that the invocation at the upcoming Dolphins game could be dedicated to the subject of terrorism, and that since it was going to be broadcast on prime-time television it would serve as an excellent means of grabbing the attention of a national audience. Since I had a close relationship with Joe Robbie, I was asked to call him. Joe asked me to come over and see him in person.

"I was in Munich for the games, Sol," he began. "When this tragedy occurred, I was devastated. All the way home, I had a terrible feeling of frustration that there was nothing I could do. And here you call me with a suggestion for something I can do, namely dedicate the invocation to that tragedy. I would like you to deliver the prayer."

I told him that I would be honored, except that the game was scheduled for Rosh Hashanah, which would prevent me from participating. I reminded him that earlier in the year, when the football schedule came out, that game was scheduled for Friday night, which coincided with the first night of Rosh Hashanah. I asked him if he could reschedule the game. He called me the next day and said that after checking with the Minnesota Vikings (the team we were to play) Pete Roselle, the NFL commissioner, and CBS, which was to broadcast the game on its national network, he was able to reschedule the game for Saturday night. I had to tell him, embarrassingly, that Rosh Hashanah is a two-day holiday.

"When can we play?" he asked.

"Sunday night after nine p.m.," I said.

Joe called back an hour later and told me that because of the CBS television schedule the best he could do was Sunday night at six p.m.. I thanked him for his efforts, and although it would still be Rosh Hashanah at that hour the Jewish fans would be very appreciative.

Since kick-off time would still fall on Rosh Hashanah, it meant I could not give the prayer concerning the Munich massacre. Joe contacted Reverend Edward Graham, a prominent African-American minister who had originally been scheduled to deliver the invocation. He suggested that the theme should be the terrorism in Munich. Subsequently, the prayer was broadcast in a very solemn and reverential tone on CBS and was extremely well received.

Soon after, Joe invited my two sons, Elliot and Jeffrey, and me to travel with him and the Dolphins to face the Jets in New York. It turned out to be not only a wonderful experience but a historic one, too, since that year was the first and so far the only "perfect season" in professional football history, when the Dolphins went 17-0 and won the Super Bowl.

On the way back, Jeffrey, who was 12 years old at the time, went around the plane collecting autographs from as many players as he could. When we came home, he asked me to photocopy the autographs. One of his classmates paid him 50 cents for a copy of the autographs sheets. Jeffrey, on his way to becoming a young entrepreneur, told me that his friend got his father to make a copy of the copy and he sold it for 75 cents. Maybe my son will run his own team one day.

The following season, we spent Thanksgiving Day in Dallas, as guests of Joe Robbie as the Dolphins faced the Cowboys. It was also November 22nd, the 10th anniversary of the assassination of President John Kennedy. We toured the area and participated in a very moving memorial service. The Dolphins won the game and went on to win the Super Bowl for the second year in a row.

For me, football was more than merely fulfilling an obligation as a clergy to deliver invocations at home games. I was a fan, and outside of the Bar Mitzvah ritual, there's nothing greater for a father to share with his sons than a professional football game.

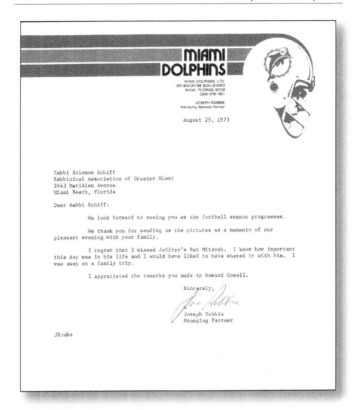

I first met the Hall of Fame coach Don Shula on December 20, 1970, when I delivered the invocation at the Miami Dolphins–Buffalo Bills game. The Dolphins won, sending them to their first post-season playoff game. That was followed by three consecutive Super Bowl appearances, with the Dolphins winning the last two.

Coach Shula's arrival in Miami created a new sense of pride and togetherness in our community. Previously, when Miamians were asked where they lived, most answered, Chicago, New York, Philadelphia, etc. The Shula era made people more likely to proudly respond, "Miami." Through his dynamic character and championship performance, on and off the field, Don Shula has served as a very positive role model, especially to our young people.

I had the good fortune of delivering the invocation at three of Coach Shula's career coaching milestones:

Win #100—October 5, 1972, against the San Diego Chargers, 24–10.

Win #300—September 22, 1991, against the Green Bay Packers, 16–13.

Win #324—October 31, 1993, against the Kansas City Chiefs, 30–10, tying Don Shula with George Halas as the winningest coach in professional football.

After returning from the "perfect season" Super Bowl victory, Coach Shula was asked by a reporter, "Now that you completed a perfect season, winning 17–0, what do you do for an encore?" To which the coach responded, "What's wrong with 34–0?" Although the Dolphins didn't quite reach that level of perfection, they did win the Super Bowl the next year.

Coach Shula was honored numerous times by various civic and community organizations, including having a street and a highway named after him. These honors reflect the deep love and appreciation of a grateful community for what Don Shula has accomplished in his storied career and for his high moral and civic ideals.

With Don Shula, Hall of Fame coach of the Miami Dolphins, in 2011, showing off the perfect season Super Bowl ring

Ten years later, in 1983, the Dolphins again went to the Super Bowl and Joe Robbie invited me to join him on his plane to California for the big game. On the return flight, he introduced me to one of his friends.

"Rabbi Schiff always brings us good luck," Joe said. "What's your record with us, Rabbi?"

"12–1," I said. I knew it easily because I kept a record at home of all the scores of the games in which I had given a prayer.

"Your record with the Dolphins is better than the Dolphins," he said, laughing. "What happened to the one game you lost?"

"I'll tell you, Joe," I began. "The way the Dolphins played that day, G-d himself couldn't have helped them."

"Well, Rabbi, I must say," Joe added. "If the Dolphins would have prepared their defense as well as yours, they would have won."

In 1985, Shirley and I were invited to travel on Joe Robbie's plane to Super Bowl XIX, once again in California. The Dolphins were playing the San Francisco 49ers. As we arrived on the tarmac, the place was swarming with media. One of the television reporters noticed my yarmulke and was curious why I was traveling with the Dolphins. He saw it as the making of an unusual story and asked me for an interview. Eventually, he asked me who I thought would win, the team from Florida or the one from California. As a guest and a clergy, I did my best to be diplomatic.

"Do you know what the abbreviation for California—CALIF—stands for?" I asked him. "Come Live In Florida. So, the team from Florida will surely beat the one from California."

We won the first half, but ended up losing the game. As Shirley always says, "They should quit while they're ahead."

That trip to the Super Bowl in San Francisco was a last-minute adventure. Joe Robbie had informed me that he might not know if there was room on his plane until the day before the scheduled departure. I packed a suitcase Wednesday night (the plane was leaving Thursday after-noon), just to be prepared in case I got the call. While I was making rounds at Jackson Memorial Hospital, I got an emergency call from my secretary, telling me that Joe Robbie had two seats for me available on his plane and he needed my decision within the hour.

I called Shirley.

"Quick!" I said. "Pack a suitcase. We're going to the Super Bowl!"

"We can't go," she said. "Jeffrey is sick."

I could hear Jeffrey in the background, saying that he wanted to go. Of course he did!

"If he's well enough to go, he's not that sick," I said.

Our other sons, Elliot and Steven, had spent the past week checking with me constantly, each pleading his case to go. Steven had the best argument:

"You already took Elli and Jeffrey on two flights on Joe Robbie's plane and you never took me (he had always been too young)."

"I have three children and one wife," I began explaining over the phone. "Since I can't pick one of my sons over the others, so the most logical choice would be Mom."

Shirley and I joined Joe Robbie and his entourage and we took off to California for Super Bowl XIX. We had a marvelous time and came home with a lot of Super Bowl memorabilia for the boys and a ton of pleasant memories.

My apologies to Stevie. I hope one day he will forgive me.

I should share one other story so no one will think I am a football snob at the expense of baseball. The Florida Marlins scheduled the opening game of the debut season of their major league baseball franchise

Super Bowl, 1973

on Monday night, April 5, 1993, which coincided with the first Passover Seder.

I called the team president to inform him of the conflict and requested a change to accommodate the many Jewish fans in Miami. He told me the date had been set for some time and it could not be changed. I suggested that they move up the start of the game from 7 p.m. to 1 p.m. He accepted my suggestion and changed the time. The change was announced in the *Miami Herald* and enabled many Jewish fans to attend.

After Joe Robbie died in 1990, I continued my relationship with the Dolphins. Wayne Huizenga, the new Dolphins owner, invited me to do a number of invocations. One season, when the Dolphins were struggling at 0-3, Mr. Huizenga approached me as I was standing on the field, waiting to be introduced.

"Rabbi, we need you to give a winning prayer."

I gave him a serious look.

"You pay Jay Fiedler (the quarterback at the time) ten million dollars a year, and you're looking to me to win the game?" Wayne burst out laughing.

"Rabbi, if we win the game, I'll give you all the credit."

I must say I gave a winning prayer, but the Dolphins lost.

In September 21, 2003, I gave the invocation at the Miami Dolphins–Buffalo Bills football game at Pro Player Stadium. As I was about to leave a pre-game tailgate party for the game, I asked the group to pray that I would give a winning prayer.

"Pray that the Dolphins win," one in the group said. "But that they don't beat the point spread." The bookies had the Dolphins listed as three-point favorites.

"How do I pray, 'Dear G-d, let the Dolphins win, but that they don't win the point spread?'" I asked incredulously. "That would make G-d some kind of divine bookie."

"Sol, you're the rabbi. You figure it out," another said, laughing.

"I'll pray that the Dolphins win," I replied. "Let G-d figure out the point spread."

The Dolphins won 17–7.

So that's not only how I came to pray for the Miami Dolphins. It's also how I came to cherish the sport of football, my friendship with Joe Robbie and his family, Coach Don Shula, the Dolphins organization, and all the fans I encountered over all these years.

Now, if we can only win another Super Bowl.

One side effect of serving in such a public position is the amount of phone calls that seem to come in on a daily basis, except for Shabbat, of course. For many years, I used a live answering service.

One day, as a few people in my office were joking about my preparation for Christmas, someone suggested I call my service. I dialed my number and the operator answered, but not at all as I expected.

"Merry Christmas, Rabbi Schiff's service," she said so cheerfully. I wanted to stop her from using this embarrassing message but not look like I was demeaning Christmas.

"You know, this time of year people are terribly busy," I said. "So please just say, 'Rabbi Schiff's service.'"

A few days later, some people began needling me (again) and suggested I call my service.

"Rabbi Schiff's service," the operator answered, just as I had asked.

"Can I speak with Rabbi Schiff?" I asked, just to amuse my colleagues. I even put the phone on speaker so everyone could hear.

"Oh, sorry," replied the operator. "Rabbi Schiff is very busy during the Christmas season."

The next day, I installed an answering machine.

8

Nixon Speaks Hebrew and Other Celebrity Encounters

I GAVE THE INVOCATION at the National Convention of the AFL-CIO in Miami Beach in 1972. Although we all were struggling with how we felt about the war in Vietnam, it was still exciting to be hosting President Richard Nixon, who was scheduled to speak at that session. Whether you agreed with his policies or not, it was always a thrill to meet such a man in person.

Our son, Jeffrey, had recently received the Presidential Physical Fitness Award for Excellence in Sports. The certificate had a machine signature of the president. I took it with me on the chance that I could get the president's personal signature. After my prayer and Nixon's speech, he walked into the crowd to shake hands. I followed him. As he turned around to leave, he practically bumped into me. I told him that my son, Jeffrey, had received the award and that it would be an honor for my son to have the president's personal signature. Nixon was glad to oblige. I gave him my ballpoint pen. With nothing to lean on, he couldn't get it to work. He handed me back my pen and took out his own—with his name on it, of course. Naturally, his worked. He asked me about Jeffrey. I described some things about him and announced that he would soon have his Bar Mitzvah. The president said, "Jeffrey sounds like a fine young man. Please give him my pen as my Bar Mitzvah gift." Before I realized what had just happened, Nixon left the room. An omen? Perhaps.

(This story first appeared in the *Miami Herald*.)

Two years later, as the antiwar movement was reaching its highest level of activity and not long before he resigned in shame, President Nixon chose Cedars of Lebanon Hospital in Miami to deliver an address on his healthcare bill. It was Valentine's Day 1974, an odd coincidence for such a presentation, but a sensible place to woo Jewish voters.

During the course of his remarks, Nixon said, "My Quaker grandmother used the word charity. The Catholics use the word caring. The Jewish people have

the best word, which is 'jedaka.'" He mispronounced
Tzedakah, meaning charity.

As Nixon finished his speech and was shaking
hands in the audience, he spotted me, and I could see
he was anxious to get through the crowd to reach me.

"How did you like my Hebrew pronunciation?" the
president asked. I was in a catch-22 situation, especially
standing next to a few of my most esteemed colleagues.
Saying Nixon's Hebrew was fine could make me look
ignorant. To say it was wrong might leave me on his
enemy list. (I only subsequently learned how long that
list already was.)

With the merits of moderation in mind, I said, "For
a Quaker, it was perfect."

Nixon was genuinely pleased.

His wife, Pat, then said to me with pride, "Rabbi,
tell your congregants that their president speaks Hebrew
very well."

(This story also appeared in the *Miami Herald*.)

A year later, at a Greater Miami Jewish Federation dinner,
I was asked to give the invocation and make the *Hamotzi*
prayer over the challah. The guest speaker was President
Gerald Ford. Once again, the Jewish voters of Miami were
being courted for another upcoming election.

Before giving the invocation, I asked the audience to rise. I approached the president and handed him a piece of challah.

"I must be the only person to ever tell a president when to get up," I said to him.

He laughed heartily and thanked me for the blessed bread. I smiled as the Secret Service man continued staring blankly ahead as I nervously took a bite of challah.

President Richard Nixon in 1973 at an AFL-CIO convention in Miami Beach, where I delivered the invocation

THE WHITE HOUSE

WASHINGTON

December 23, 1971

Dear Rabbi Schiff:

It was thoughtful of you to write as you did on
December 6 following my appearance at the AFL-
CIO Convention, and I am particularly pleased to
have the picture which you enclosed of our meeting on that occasion.

You must be very proud of your son, Jeffrey,
and I am delighted that I had the pleasure of
meeting him when I was in Miami. I look forward to seeing both of you again on my future
trips to Florida.

Your prayers on behalf of my family and me are
deeply appreciated, and this note comes to you
with my thanks and warmest good wishes for the
New Year.

Sincerely,

Richard Nixon

Rabbi Solomon Schiff
Executive Vice President
   and Director of Chaplaincy
Rabbinical Association of Greater Miami
2443 Meridian Avenue
Miami Beach, Florida

The privileges and responsibilities of serving in an administrative position as a rabbi meant that I had the occasional opportunity to meet some foreign dignitaries. Once, Shirley and I were invited to have dinner with King Juan Carlos II and Queen Sofia of Spain.

I came home excited to tell Shirley the news.

"When is it?" she asked.

"Monday night, April 2nd." I replied.

"We can't go," she said. "We have our meditation class that night."

"What? You'd choose a 'snooze fest' over dinner with a king?" I asked incredulously.

Shirley held firm.

"We have a commitment," she said firmly.

"Fine," I said. "But remember what happened the last time a king invited a woman to come to his party and she refused." I reminded her of the biblical story of Purim, when Queen Vashti refused the invitation of King Achashveros to attend his party. He subsequently had her executed.

"I guess we'd better go," Shirley said, shrugging her shoulders.

In the coming days, many articles appeared in the local paper about the king's approaching visit. One story in particular talked about etiquette when meeting with the king. It said that if one gets the opportunity of talking directly to the king then one should definitely not say anything negative about Spain.

"I guess that means I can't mention the expulsion of the Jews," I said to Shirley.

She shrugged her shoulders and rolled her eyes.

The article then stated that you should say something positive about Spain.

"I guess I could say 'The Jews had a marvelous time in Spain, until they were kicked out.'"

A few days later, as we lined up for our meeting with the king and queen, someone in front of me asked, "What can I talk to him about? I don't know anything complimentary about Spain."

"Tell him you love Spanish omelets," I offered. He laughed and spread my comment along the reception line. As Dade County Mayor Alex Pinelis formally introduced us to the king and queen, we had time only to take a photo with the royal couple and the mayor. During dinner, when we spotted the royal couple sitting alone, we decided to go over and talk with them.

I mentioned to the king that when I had visited Spain, I went to a small synagogue on the third floor of an apartment building in Madrid. Outside in the hallway was a model of a new synagogue they were planning to construct, which they did in fact build later on.

"This was to be the first synagogue that was built in Spain since" (I was hesitant to finish my sentence, but I did, adding) "since the Jews were expelled from Spain."

We all waited for his response.

"That was a terrible mistake," the king said, without hesitation.

To lighten the moment, I mentioned that we had recently met with the president of Germany.

"Oh, Johannes Rau is a good friend of mine," the king said.

Our conversation soon grew quite casual and I ended up inviting the king and queen to stay in our home on their next visit to Miami.

"Of course, we don't live in a palace as you do," I said.

"I'll let you in on a secret," the king said, his eyes twinkling. "I don't live in one, either."

"In that case," I said. "You will feel right at home in our house."

In May 1980, President Jimmy Carter invited a number of Jewish community leaders from around the country, myself included, to the White House, where he honored Israel's prime minister, Menachem Begin. After socializing with the invited guests, the two heads of state addressed the assembly.

President Carter made two historic commitments: first, that the United States would set aside land in Washington, D.C., to build a Holocaust Memorial

Museum; second, that the United States would make "Days of Remembrance" an annual rite to coincide with Yom Hashoa, the day of remembering for the six million Jews exterminated by the Nazis.

Both of these commitments have been fulfilled. A magnificent Holocaust Memorial Museum was built on government land near the Capitol Mall. It has become our nation's tribute to the Jewish victims of the Holocaust, visited by hundreds of thousands of people of all faiths, to learn, through sight and sound, of the horrible atrocities that took place during World War II. An annual ceremony has been held in the rotunda of the Capitol since 1980. We have Carter to thank for this milestone and how it's been perpetuated.

With President Jimmy Carter in 1980

In August 2000, Shirley and I were invited to a reception with Vice President Al Gore and his running mate, Senator Joe Lieberman.

I introduced myself to Lieberman with the words, "Sholom Aleichem," to which he responded, "Aleichem Sholom." I told him how proud I was that one of our own had made it to such a high position.

"The only thing I can say," Lieberman replied, "is Boruch Hashem" (Thank the Lord). Later, when he was introduced to speak, the emcee said, "I give you the one who will be the next vice president of the United States.

"Im yirtze Hashem," I said, G-D willing. Senator Lieberman nodded to me in agreement.

"You know, Senator," I then said to him, "I have a picture with four U.S. presidents, and I would like to have a picture with you as our sixth—after Gore, of course.

"Chop nisht," he said. (Not so fast.)

After the photographer took a picture of Lieberman, Shirley, and myself, Vice President Gore came by. I told him about my four presidential pictures and how we would like him to become the fifth. He happily obliged and then spoke to the group.

"There is an old Yiddish saying," he began, "which I'm sure I will mispronounce. The word is 'Tuchiss'" (Yiddish for "behind" as in "tush").

Lieberman corrected him by saying, "You mean, 'Tachliss' (straight to the point), not 'Tuchiss.'"

As everybody was joking about Gore's charming gaff, I raised my hand to get his attention.

"Oh, my rabbi is going to correct me," Gore said.

"You tuk les and do more," I said, hoping he got my play on words.

Gore and Lieberman nodded approvingly. I later told Lieberman that our children live in Stamford, Connecticut, and doven (pray) in Rabbi Joel Ehrenkranz's synagogue. He said Rabbi Ehrenkranz had Bar Mitzvah'd him. He inquired about the names of our boys and said he would look forward to meeting them.

At a rally some months later in Coral Gables, I brought a letter, which I addressed to Al Gore and in which I had written, "Your selection of Joe Lieberman, which is the first time a Jew has been chosen as a vice-presidential candidate, is in keeping with a statement by George Washington. In a letter to the Hebrew Congregation of Newport, Rhode Island, in 1790, he wrote, 'For happily the government of the United States, which gives to bigotry no sanction, to persecution no assistance, requires only that they who live under its protection should demean themselves as good citizens.' The letter proclaims that all citizens are equal. Your selection, Mr. Gore, reiterates that principle."

As I handed Gore the letter, he noticed my name on the envelope.

"Schiff; my son-in-law's name is Schiff."

He asked his security men to find his son-in-law to meet Shirley and me. Gore told me that his son-in-law was related to Jacob Schiff (the well-known philanthropist). I said I, too, was related to a Jacob Schiff (my brother). His son-in-law was excited to meet us. We talked about his new baby and took pictures with him. He said that if Gore were elected, he would invite us to the White House.

Unfortunately, our home state didn't quite make that possible.

When Congresswoman Ileana Ros-Lehtinen of Miami first ran for the U.S. Congress, she invited me to attend one of her campaign meetings. She expressed her gratitude for my attendance. We immediately developed a friendship and an appreciation for each other's views.

In 1998, after she was reelected, she instituted a very unusual ceremony. In addition to the usual swearing-in ceremony in the Capitol in Washington, D.C., she initiated a swearing-in ceremony in Miami, as well. She invited her constituents and political and community leaders to the event. She had a federal judge conduct the ceremony, in which several other members of Congress were sworn in as well.

Mrs. Lehtinen invited me to offer a prayer. After the ceremony, she asked me whether I had ever given a prayer in the U.S. Congress. I said I had given a prayer in the U.S. Senate, but not in the Congress. She said she would recommend that I be invited to do so. The House Chaplain, to whom she wrote, responded that there was a long waiting list.

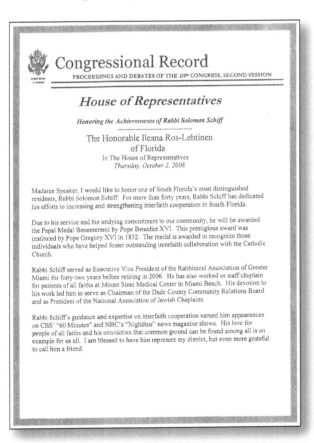

Congressional Record
PROCEEDINGS AND DEBATES OF THE *110th* CONGRESS, SECOND SESSION

House of Representatives

Honoring the Achievements of Rabbi Solomon Schiff

The Honorable Ileana Ros-Lehtinen
of Florida
In The House of Representatives
Thursday, October 2, 2008

Madame Speaker, I would like to honor one of South Florida's most distinguished residents, Rabbi Solomon Schiff. For more than forty years, Rabbi Schiff has dedicated his efforts to increasing and strengthening interfaith cooperation in South Florida.

Due to his service and his undying commitment to our community, he will be awarded the Papal Medal Benemerenti by Pope Benedict XVI. This prestigious award was instituted by Pope Gregory XVI in 1832. The medal is awarded to recognize those individuals who have helped foster outstanding interfaith collaboration with the Catholic Church.

Rabbi Schiff served as Executive Vice President of the Rabbinical Association of Greater Miami for forty-two years before retiring in 2006. He has also worked as staff chaplain for patients of all faiths at Mount Sinai Medical Center in Miami Beach. His devotion to his work led him to serve as Chairman of the Dade County Community Relations Board and as President of the National Association of Jewish Chaplains.

Rabbi Schiff's guidance and expertise on interfaith cooperation earned him appearances on CBS' "60 Minutes" and NBC's "Nightline" news magazine shows. His love for people of all faiths and his conviction that common ground can be found among all is an example for us all. I am blessed to have him represent my district, but even more grateful to call him a friend.

It was a great honor to appear before Congress

A year later, on July 29, 1999, a *Miami Herald* reporter contacted me in my Washington, D.C., hotel, the night before I was to deliver my second prayer at the U.S. Senate. In the course of our conversation she said, "I understand you may have a conflict tomorrow because you are giving a prayer in the U.S. Senate on the same day as the circumcision ceremony of your grandson, in Stamford, Connecticut. What will happen if the timing is such that you cannot attend both?"

"Well, I must be at my grandson's circumcision ceremony," I began. "But at the same time, I must be in the Senate chamber because without me, they won't have a prayer."

The timing worked out fine and I was able to attend both.

Two years later, Mrs. Lehtinen invited me again to offer a prayer at her local swearing-in ceremony. Since there was a change in chaplains in the House of Representatives, she told me she would make a request of the new chaplain. Within a short time, I received a letter from the chaplain, the first Catholic chaplain in the U.S. Congress, inviting me to offer a prayer on July 12, 2001.

Shirley and I arranged to have our entire family join us in Washington for this meaningful, historic event.

The Schiff Family with Florida Congresswoman Ileana
Ros-Lehtinen, outside the Capitol in Washington, D.C., 2001

As we approached the hall of the House of Representatives, our oldest grandson, eight-year-old Mikey, grabbed me tightly.

"Zaidie, are you scared?" he asked.

"No, Mikey," I said. "Because I've made such speeches many times and I practiced what I am going to say now. When you are asked to make a speech, if you practice and gain experience, you won't be scared, either."

When I arrived at the podium, and as we waited for the session to begin, I chatted with the clerk of the House. I told her of Mikey's question, and my answer.

"Do you know who spoke at this podium where you are going to offer your prayer?" she asked, smiling.

She had me stumped for the moment.

"Winston Churchill, Conrad Adenauer, and Charles De Gaulle for a start," she said. "General Douglas MacArthur gave his famous farewell address right here and nearly every American president's State of the Union address has happened right here where you are standing."

"Okay, now I'm scared," I responded.

Later that day, I told someone about the clerk's comments.

"In the future," he said, "when clerks make this comment to some other nervous person about to address Congress, they will add, 'and Rabbi Solomon Schiff.'"

With President Bill Clinton, 1994

On April 23, 2009, my wife, Shirley, and I were invited to attend a ceremony at the Capitol. I was invited as the new chairman of the Holocaust Memorial of the Greater Miami Jewish Federation in Miami Beach. President Barack Obama addressed the group, consisting mostly of Holocaust survivors. He mentioned that his grandfather had been an American soldier who took part in liberating one of the Nazi death camps. He expressed his deep sympathy for the victims and their survivors;

stressing that only through remembering the past can we help ensure that this tragedy never occurs again.

Obama's statement is in keeping with the prophetic words of George Santayana: "Those who do not learn from history are condemned to repeat it." What an honor it has been for me to play even a small role in making this happen.

With so much talk about the Tea Party these days, perhaps the Tea Party should take a coffee break.

9
Adventures in Israel

ONE DAY, WHILE SHIRLEY AND I were visiting the Israeli Museum in Jerusalem, we came upon a mobile type of artwork. It consisted of about twenty thin, steel rods hanging from the ceiling, with steel balls connected at the bottom of each of them. When you pushed a button, an electric charge sent the balls moving back and forth.

When it stopped, I touched one of the balls to feel its substance. Shirley chastised me for doing that. Within a few minutes, someone came over and pushed the button. All the balls started to move in one direction—all except the one I had just touched. It lagged a little behind the others. As the balls returned, they hit the slower one, which threw the balls off kilter until each one ended up flying in different directions. The people watching this artwork grew confused, seemingly wondering what a strange mobile it was, with no rhyme or reason for its function.

"I told you not to touch it," Shirley said. I moved away, hoping no one had seen me perform such mischief.

Many years later, I had lunch with the Israeli Consul General of Israel to Miami. During our conversation, I mentioned this story.

"So you're the one who fouled up that whole exhibit," he said. He was joking, I think. I hope. I since learned that Do Not Touch means Do Not Touch!

This was similar to another experience I had in Israel during a rabbinic mission soon after the Yom Kippur War. We had come across many destroyed tanks. Everyone was picking up souvenirs. I picked up a piece of metal that had a switch on it. I kept it, carrying it all the way back to the States with a real feeling of pride.

In showing this item to many people over the years, I explained that this was a switch that fired the tank's cannon. This story was always received with great interest. Once, after relaying my experience to a group of friends, someone who had actually served in an American tank division said that the trigger used to fire the cannon is a button and not a switch. He pointed out that the switch is used to turn the lights on and off. I never was able to tell my story that way again. At least I didn't break the switch.

With Israeli Prime Minister Yitzchak Rabin and his wife at an Israel Bonds dinner at the Fontainebleau Hotel

Once while on a Jewish Federation mission to Israel, Shirley and I went to a shopping mall in Jerusalem, where we saw a Burger King that was kosher. Since there are no kosher Burger Kings in the United States, we decided to eat our first hamburger in a fast food joint. When we returned to our hotel, we excitedly told our friends that we had eaten a kosher hamburger at a Burger King.

"How does it compare to our hamburgers back in the States?" one of our friends asked.

"You are not going to get me to answer that question," I said, refusing to fall for such a trick.

Shirley and I were invited by longtime dear friends, Stanley and Lenore Weinstein, to be their guests on a trip to Israel to officiate at their son Moshe's wedding.

Two unusual things happened during that experience. We arrived in Israel on Hoshanah Rabbah, the last day of the holiday of Sukkoth. We took along a Lulov and Etrog set to be used on the plane traveling to Israel. (These are elements of nature that are used in service on the Sukkoth holiday). As we entered Ben Gurion Airport in Israel, a representative of the Agriculture Department confiscated our Lulov. When I asked him why, he said they had found some foreign bugs in some of the Lulovim that had just been brought in to the country. They were not bugs grown in Israel. I guess the Israelis discriminate against foreign bugs. It might be that they thought my Lulov was bugged—no pun intended (or maybe there is).

Shirley reminded me of a story she had once heard about an Arab wandering in the desert, dying of thirst. He came upon a Jew with a commercial stand.

"Can you sell me some water," the Arab said. "I'm terribly thirsty."

The Jew replied, "I don't sell water. I sell ties."

"Who needs a tie?" the other man said. "I need water."

So the owner of the tie stand said, "If you walk several miles in that direction, you will run into a restaurant owned by my brother. There you can get water."

After a few hours, the man returned, his tongue hanging out of his mouth, in even worse condition than before.

"Did you find the restaurant, and did you get the water?" the Jewish man asked.

"No," the Arab gentleman replied. "They wouldn't let me in without a tie."

Shirley shrugged and said, "I'll bet outside the terminal, the agricultural representative has a brother selling Lulovim."

The next unusual thing Shirley and I discovered on that trip was at the wedding, where about half the men were carrying weapons tucked into their trousers or in holsters dangling from their waists.

As we were dancing a fast and raucous dance, the man in front of me was jumping up and down, dancing enthusiastically, with gusto. He was wearing a machine gun slung around his back. Every time he jumped, the gun kept hitting me. I was quite nervous, and sweating bullets (no pun intended). I tapped him on the shoulder and asked softly, "Would you mind if we danced a waltz?" When I didn't succeed, I changed places in the dance line, removing what I hoped was my only chance of any immediate danger.

In 1972, Shirley and I were part of a mission to Israel, entitled "Communication of Values." A CBS television crew planned to show some of the conference on their network program *Look Up and Live*, so they accompanied a number of rabbis who represented various American boards of rabbis.

We stayed in the newly opened hotel Moriah. Although it was a kosher hotel, the overall spirit of the staff was not religiously sensitive. At Shabbat dinner,

With Israeli President Shimon Peres in 1984

for example, as we were singing traditional Friday night Zemiros, we were asked by some of the staff to stop singing, as we were disturbing the other guests.

Kosher hotels always provide complimentary wine to their guests for the Kiddush prayer. In this case, the waiters insisted that we purchase the wine and sign for it. We argued with the manager that signing on the Sabbath was strictly forbidden and that kosher hotels always provide free wine for the Kiddush ceremony. He agreed to give us a single glass of wine for the entire table. We insisted that each one of us receive a glass of wine, to which he finally agreed.

Not long after, the head of the CBS crew, Chalmers (Chum) Dale, a good Irish Christian, entered the dining room.

I whispered to him, "Say to your waiter the word, 'kiddush.'"

Without knowing what it meant since he was not Jewish, Chum said the word and received a complimentary glass of wine. He later commented that this was like receiving manna from heaven.

In 1973, following the Yom Kippur War, we had a rabbinic mission to Israel. I called my cousin Chashi Genauer who lives in Israel, to say hello and to invite her and her husband to visit with me Saturday night in our hotel, the Tel Aviv Hilton. During their visit, she asked me why they brought the rabbis to Israel. I answered that they wanted us to see how the Israelis live.

"If they want you to see how the Israelis live," she began, "why do they bring you to the Hilton? If they want you to see how the Israelis live, they should bring you to my house."

"The only incentive we had to come to Israel was that they promised us the Hilton," I said. "If they brought us all to your house, no one would come."

In 1976, my wife, Shirley, and I participated in a Jewish Federation mission to Israel. The final event was a march to the Western Wall. An exciting program was presented on a stage next to the Wall, including a dozen rabbis sounding the shofar (ram's horn), singing, and praying. The program ended with a message of greeting from the Speaker of the Knesset.

The speaker, Yitzchak Shamir, was a very short man. His speech consisted of the following:

"Welcome to Israel."

This was the shortest speech I had ever heard.

"No wonder he's the Speaker of the Knesset," I said. "Short in content to go with his height."

In a few years, Shamir was elected as Israel's prime minister. Despite his short speeches, Yitzchak Shamir became one of Israel's most effective and "tallest" prime ministers.

With Israeli Prime Minister Yitzchak Shamir in 1987

With Chaim Herzog in 1991 at the
president's residence in Jerusalem

Each and every one of our trips to Israel has special meaning for me. First of all, sharing these experiences with Shirley has been wonderful beyond words. Perhaps even deeper than that, if there ever could be such a thing, is the feeling I carry for my father, and how it would have been his dream to set foot one day in the land of our fathers. How lucky I have been for all these reasons.

America is often referred to as a "melting pot." To me, this implies putting all the food in one pot, boiling away all the differences, and ending up with one uniform hash. I prefer the term "dinner plate." You have meat, potatoes, and vegetables, each with its own color, nutritional value, and taste. Together they make an interesting, attractive, and exciting meal. So are the benefits of diversity, which we should teach as a blessing and not a curse. This is the essence of the interfaith mission.

10
My Life in the Interfaith Community

THE FIRST NATIONAL CONFERENCE on Faith-based and Community Initiatives was held at the White House on June 1, 2004. I was invited as a member of the Florida Advisory Board. After responding that I would attend, I received a call from the White House, inviting me to offer the opening prayer. Of course I was very honored, but I was even more curious to know how I was selected from over 1,000 religious leaders from around the country. When I asked Jim Towey, the White House Director of the Office of Faith-based and Community Initiatives, he said that he recommended me to the president since he had worked with me on various Florida commissions.

The conference was a huge success. President Bush gave an impassioned speech and I had a chance to meet and speak with him about a few different subjects.

"I want to thank you, Mr. President, for your strong support of Israel."

"It's the right thing to do," he replied.

The president was in the middle of his reelection campaign and Florida was expected to be a critical state, as it had certainly been in 2000. Bush immediately asked that a picture be taken of both of us.

"Did you get it?" he said anxiously to the cameraman. "Take another one."

The photograph was published, together with a story about the conference. In the article, Jim Towey said, "The president appreciated Rabbi Schiff's participation and was thrilled to have the chance to visit with him during the conference."

My work with various interfaith groups began decades ago. It's always been a priority for me to reach out beyond the borders of the Jewish community and try to improve relations with others. I like to think that this work has made a difference by increasing mutual understanding between people of different faiths as well as multiplying humanitarian efforts to make the world a better place.

With George W. Bush at the White House, 2005

In July 1967, one month after the Six Day War, my wife and I were part of an interfaith mission to Israel. From there, we traveled to Rome. I carried a very small Bible, the size of a thumbnail. The Catholic priest who accompanied us asked to borrow the Bible in order to show it to the curator of the Vatican museum. He later told me that the curator said that if I would donate this Judaic work to the Vatican, I would receive a thank you letter signed by the Pope, himself. I was in a quandary as to what to do. To get such a high honor from the Pope is extremely rare and would be cherished for a lifetime. On the other hand, the guilt I would probably feel afterward from giving a Jewish treasure to the Church could also last a lifetime. I decided to forego the honor and keep the Bible. It was one of the few times I let my personal choice outweigh the bigger picture.

On August 6, 1970, while on an interfaith mission to Japan, I was getting a haircut in a barbershop in Hiroshima. I was quite nervous. I asked the barber not to use a razor. It was the 25th anniversary of the dropping of the first atomic bomb so it was a very emotional time for the Japanese and the Americans, especially those in Japan, sitting vulnerably in a chair as their old "enemy" stood behind them with a sharp scissor in hand.

We visited the Cenotaph, a memorial to the victims, where about 80,000 names are inscribed. Every year on the anniversary, they add additional names of those who died during that year.

I also visited patients in the Atomic Bomb Hospital who were victims of the atomic blast, still suffering its effects so many years later. At first, this seemed surprising, but when I learned more about the horrors of atomic warfare, it wasn't shocking; it was merely devastating. The stark reality left an indelible impression on me.

During my stay at the Royal Osaka Hotel, we were pleasantly surprised to hear that Emperor Hirohito was staying at the same hotel while visiting Expo '70. I found out what floor he was staying on. I asked a clerk to write a note for me in Japanese, which I dictated to her in English.

"My name is Rabbi Solomon Schiff from Miami, Florida. I have come to bring greetings to the Emperor from all the Jews in Florida."

The clerk was shocked. She couldn't believe I actually was going to visit the Emperor. As the elevator stopped at his floor, I quickly stepped out and discovered two burly guards stationed by the elevator (I guess to keep people like me from entering the floor). I handed them my note. They argued with me in halting English, insisting that I could not see the Emperor. They called another official who told me the same thing. I protested politely, saying I was leaving the next day.

"If the Emperor doesn't see me now, he won't ever see me," I said, knowing full well how silly that must have sounded.

They finally brought out a public relations type person.

"The Emperor is very happy you are here. He extends to you and the Florida Jews his best wishes, but he is very tired and not up to company."

The next morning, as our group was preparing to leave the hotel, security men cordoned off the lobby in preparation for the Emperor's departure. They rolled out a red carpet and the lobby soon filled with excited spectators. Reverend Luther Pierce, one of our group leaders, asked a security man whether it is permitted to snap a picture of the Emperor. He said, "not with a flash." Since I had a flash camera, I moved to the other side, behind a Japanese contingent, in order to be removed from the inquisitive Reverend. As the Emperor walked out of the elevator down the red carpet, I snapped his picture. As the people in front of me turned around to see where the flash came from, I also turned around. As they turned back, I snapped another picture, getting a picture of the Emperor facing me. As the Emperor and his party left the hotel, Reverend Pierce ran over to me.

"If it comes out," he said excitedly. "I'd like a copy."

Before I left the hotel in Osaka, a strange thing happened. As the Emperor was about to leave and we were confined to the lobby, I left my luggage nearby with my hat on top of it. Once the Emperor left, I went to retrieve my luggage and found that my hat was missing. Since the only one who had left the hotel at that moment was the Emperor, it would seem logical to suspect that he was the culprit who had taken my hat.

A number of years later, I read a newspaper story that said that the Emperor, who was visiting Washington, D.C., had joined President Ronald Reagan for dinner. As they left the restaurant, the article said, the Emperor found that his hat was missing. I always wondered whether the hat that the Emperor lost was in fact my hat.

In the early 70s, Congress was considering passing legislation that would remove the exemption from military services for Divinity students. We arranged for several clergy to visit Washington to lobby senators and congressmen to retain the exemption.

As we visited with one congressman, Rabbi Tibor Stern presented his arguments for the exemption.

"If we send our rabbinic students to the military, they will become corrupt and lose their morality."

I began pinching Rabbi Stern under the table to get him to back off. After we left the office, Rabbi Stern asked who was pinching him? I raised my hand.

"You keep saying the Army corrupts the morals of our young people. Do you know who you were talking to? That man is the chairman of the Armed Services Committee. I don't think he appreciated hearing that the Army corrupts the morals of young people."

"You think they hear everything you say?" Rabbi Stern asked.

We then visited Senator Gurney, the Republican senator from Florida. Rabbi Stern, instead of presenting the agreed-upon talking points, went off again on his unique path.

"I think the one who originated this idea of drafting Divinity students is surely a Communist who wants to destroy the moral fiber of our nation," he proclaimed.

I began pinching him again.

"Why were you pinching me?" Rabbi Stern asked as we left the senator's office.

"You referred to the originator of this legislation as a Communist, out to destroy our moral fiber," I said. "Do you know who the originator was? President Richard Nixon. And Senator Gurney is his greatest supporter."

"You think they hear everything you say?" Rabbi Stern responded (again).

I guess that despite some of our stumbling, we must have made a strong impression, because the legislation was defeated. The exemption of Divinity students from the military service, which had been in effect since the Revolutionary War, will continue uninterrupted, at least for now.

During September 1984, a clergyman named Pastor John Mellish of the Margate Church of the Nazarene, was sentenced to sixty days in jail for contempt of court because he refused to reveal a counseling conversation he'd had with one of his parishioners, who had been accused of sexually abusing a six-year-old girl and had revealed this information to Pastor Mellish.

His refusal was based on the longstanding recognition of "clergy–penitent privilege." The pastor spent one night in jail and was released while he appealed the verdict. Eventually, the court upheld his "privilege" and the case was dismissed.

During this time, an important debate was held throughout the community, with many clergy of different faiths discussing the concept of "clergy–penitent privilege." While no one could dispute the horrific act of child abuse, especially that of a sexual nature, all of us felt that the clergy–parishioner/congregant relationship should be afforded the same treatment that a client–attorney or doctor–patient privilege provides.

TIME magazine, CNN, and CBS's *60 Minutes* did segments on this issue, and all three interviewed me on the subject. In *TIME* (October 1, 1984) I stated that there is an "unbreakable bond" between clergymen and congregants that is protected by the U.S. Constitution's guarantee of religious freedom. On both CNN and *60 Minutes*, I said that it was very important for me as a clergyman to support the rights of a co-religionist "because, if one faith group is denied their rights, other faith groups, including mine, could be denied our rights." Since the case was finally adjudicated in the pastor's favor, it reinforced the time-honored constitutional protection of freedom of religion.

In 1984, Shirley and I participated in a rabbinic mission to Poland. The group assembled at Kennedy Airport for a briefing by the professionals who arranged the mission. Since Poland was then under Communist rule, they were concerned that the rabbis would engage in political conversations with the people we were to meet.

They enumerated many dos and don'ts.

"Can we ask them about Solidarity?" I said.

"Don't mention Solidarity!" The speaker snapped, reacting with obvious anger. He explained that this was a no-no. There are Communist spies everywhere and discussing this subject could jeopardize our entire mission. This prompted a reaction by the other participants. They questioned how I would even ask such a question. I quickly realized that the subject of Solidarity was not to be raised again.

We arrived in Warsaw and were taken to a hotel and immediately ushered into the dining room for dinner. Shirley and I happened to sit with the Polish tour guide.

Shirley asked the waiter for lemon.

"There is a shortage of lemons," the waiter replied.

She asked for coffee.

"We're short of coffee this month," came the waiter's reply.

We got the same answer when we asked for other foods.

"It seems like there are a lot of shortages here," I remarked to the guide.

"It's not us," he said. "It's Solidarity that caused this."

I quickly turned to my colleagues.

"He mentioned Solidarity, not me."

The fact is, that although there was great fear of mentioning that word, almost every conversation we had during our visit revolved around Solidarity. It was on everyone's mind, and the movement eventually caused the upheaval that ended not only Communism in Poland, but also the downfall of the entire Soviet dictatorship.

During a rabbinic mission to Jordan in 1994, our group had the distinct honor of being invited to meet with King Hussein. During a bus ride on the day before this historic meeting, I said to the chairman of our mission, Rabbi Haskell Bernat, that it would be appropriate for us to recite a special prayer in the king's presence.

It is a tradition that when one sees a king he should recite the following blessing:

"Blessed are you, Lord our G-d, King of the universe, who has given of His glory to a human being."

The chairman checked with some of the other rabbis who said that the only time one recites this blessing is if there are Jews living in the king's realm. Since there were no Jews living in Jordan, it would not be appropriate. The objection was mainly to the fact that in the blessing we recite G-d's name and if the prayer is not appropriate, then we would be reciting G-d's name in vain.

I then suggested that we need not use the actual name of G-d, but could use a substitute, namely Hashem, which is used when it is not appropriate to pronounce the actual name of G-d. My suggestion was brought to the group who delivered this response: If we use a substitute name of G-d, we would in effect be trying to fool the king, thus insulting him. If he should discover this subterfuge, this could have very negative consequences.

I then responded with the following observation: "I think it would be okay for us to use the substitute name of G-d, namely Hashem, and the king, even if he discovered such a replacement of G-d's name, would not be insulted, because the king is the head of the Hashemite kingdom."

This whole discussion became moot when the following morning the Jordanian newspapers headline read, "The king's cabinet has resigned," causing a national crisis needing the king's full attention for the entire day. We were informed that our meeting would have to be postponed to sometime in the evening. Since there was a deadline for our delegation to cross back into Israel, there was no way that we could meet with the king that night. That prayer controversy never had to be resolved.

On that same mission, which was held soon after a peace treaty had been signed between Israel and Jordan, tourism was flourishing, enabling us to cross back into Jordan for a tour experience. Wanting to minimize any friction between Jordanian Muslims and our Jewish delegates, we were advised that when we crossed the border into Jordan, we should remove our yarmulkes and put on regular caps or hats.

As we crossed the border, everyone did as we were instructed. The people on the bus pointed to a rabbi in the first row, laughing and making various comments. The man being laughed at asked why they were laughing at him. He was told to look at his cap.

"I don't know what the joke is," he said. "I was instructed to remove my yarmulke after crossing the border and to put on a cap, which I did."

What this rabbi hadn't realized was that his cap read, "Jewish Community Centers of South Florida." Luckily, I had an extra Miami Dolphins hat with me and lent it to our confused friend.

In March 1999, I joined a mission to Prague with NABOR, the North American Boards of Rabbis. We met with leaders of the government and of the Jewish and Catholic communities. Among the various issues that we discussed was a serious concern about an ongoing source of anti-Semitism that has been festering for several hundred years.

On the famous Charles Bridge in Prague stands a statue of Jesus with a revered verse inscribed on it in Hebrew letters made of gold. The translation of the verse goes like this:

"Holy, Holy, Holy is the Lord of Hosts: The whole earth is full of his glory" (Isaiah 6:3).

Why should such a verse be written on a statue of Jesus? Legend has it that a Jew supposedly made a disrespectful gesture by the statue. As punishment, the authorities forced the Jewish community to contribute a great sum of money. With this sum, they had that Hebrew verse engraved on the statue. This legend has been a source of much pain for the Jews of Prague and has ingloriously contributed greatly to anti-Semitism over many, many years.

After an entire year of negotiations among the representatives of NABOR, the Catholic hierarchy, and the Czech government, a 300-year-old symbol of anti-Semitism was finally exposed and rectified. On March 8, 2000, corresponding with Ash Wednesday, representatives of all three groups placed three plaques at the site of the statue—in English, Czech, and Hebrew. This transformed that ancient symbol of Christian triumph and anti-Semitism into a statement of hope and sharing for the future of Jewish-Catholic relations. The ceremony was held on the eve of Pope John Paul II's historic visit to Israel.

For me, this story reinforces the belief that the human spirit is basically good and that hope for a better day is always alive.

Interfaith work isn't only about fostering good relationships between different religious groups. Sometimes, we clergy are called upon to settle complicated and highly sensitive personal disputes.

Many years ago, a Jewish man married a Catholic woman who converted to Judaism. At one point, they got divorced and the couple shared custody of their son.

The man came to see me with a serious complaint. He told me that the mother, without his knowledge or consent, had their son baptized in a Catholic church. He was furious. The son was being raised in the Jewish tradition and enjoyed participating in Sabbath services in the synagogue. His wife, he claimed, had originally agreed to raise him as a Jew and had now violated that pledge, inflicting confusion and dissention upon their son and their family.

The man was so angry that he threatened to sue the Archdiocese of Miami for this violation of the child's religious rights. He had repeatedly contacted the Archdiocese to nullify the baptism, to no avail. I convinced him that making this a public issue would be hurtful to Catholic-Jewish relations, as well as hurtful to his cause. More important, it would be wrongfully putting his son in the middle of an adult argument.

I arranged a meeting in my office between the man and Monsignor Brian Walsh. It took all of my persuasive powers to keep the man from exploding. I suggested that the Archdiocese issue a nullification letter and that the man drop all plans for a lawsuit. They both agreed; the letter was issued, and the lawsuit proceedings were dropped.

About 20 years later, I was at a chaplaincy retreat in Miami. During the meeting, I had occasion to refer to this incident. One of my colleagues, Fr. David Smith, spoke up.

"I am the priest who performed the baptism," he volunteered. He later explained that the mother never told him the boy was Jewish and gave him no cause to refuse the baptism request.

In March 2001, Shirley and I were at a conference of the North American Boards of Rabbis (NABOR), in Berlin, Germany. Among the issues that we discussed with German government officials was the issue of restitution. The German government and its industries had agreed to pay several billion dollars in restitution to the Jews who were used as slave laborers during World War II. Each of these entities was to pay half of the total amount. The problem was that by law, the German government could not release its funds until the companies that had used Jews as slave laborers released their funds. They refused to release their portions until they were given assurance that they would not be sued by survivors in American courts. In the meantime, the survivors, who were all elderly, and many of them in dire poverty, were being deprived of their rightful payments. We met with a number of high government officials including some in the German Bundestag (Parliament), German President Johannes Rau, and German Foreign Minister Joschka Fischer, among others. We pleaded with them to change the law and allow the restitution moneys to be released.

The next morning, I was quite surprised when a BBC radio reporter interviewed me.

"How do you feel about the fact that the German government just changed the law and they will release the funds?" he asked, completely surprising me with the news.

"It's great news," I said. "And it will be a great relief for the many survivors that are elderly and ill, who will now be able to obtain funds that will help provide them with a more secure and helpful future."

We felt quite pleased that we had helped correct an enormous moral error.

In November 2004, a German television crew interviewed me about my reaction to the impending death of Yasser Arafat, chairman of the Palestine Liberation Organization. The crew was in Florida to cover the Bush–Kerry election. They'd been asked to stay on to report on the Jewish reaction to the Arafat issue.

After the interview, the cameraman shared with me that for his whole life, he had been feeling a tremendous sense of guilt about being German. He didn't know what his father or grandfather had done during the war and was troubled that they might have done something terrible connected to the Holocaust. Whenever he was asked where he came from, he answered with shame that he was from Germany. The stigma of being a citizen of a country that perpetrated the most barbaric acts in human history created an ongoing pain for him and he was looking to me to possibly relieve some of it for him.

I responded by telling him the following: In the Ten Commandments, it says, "For I am a jealous G-d, who visits the sin of fathers upon the children to the third and fourth generations" (Exodus 20:5). There is another Biblical verse, which says, "Fathers shall not be put to death because of sons and sons shall not be put to death because of fathers. Each man shall be put to death for his own sins" (Deuteronomy 24:16).

"How do we reconcile these contradictory statements?" I asked him. I went on to explain that the commentaries explain that, "sins are visited upon the children to the third and fourth generation" applies only to offspring who approve and continue the sins of the past.

I told him that if he were a skinhead, a neo-Nazi, or any other type of anti-Semite, he should feel guilty because then he would be continuing the sins of his fathers. If, however, he leads an honest life, respecting others as a decent human being, he need not have these guilty feelings any longer. In fact, his guilty feelings indicate he is ashamed of the actions of the Nazi generation and that he is attempting to make amends for that behavior.

A few weeks later, I received an email.

"I don't know if you remember me, but I want you to know that you removed a heavy stone off my chest. Thank you."

So you see, interfaith cooperation sometimes results in big changes, one person at a time.

I served as chairman of the Greater Miami Religious Leaders Coalition, an organization of clergy of different faiths. A group of Thai Buddhists came to one of our meetings. They told us that they wanted to build a

Miami interfaith mission to Israel, 2000

Buddhist Temple in the southern part of Miami, but they had been denied a zoning permit. Among the reasons they had been given for the denial were too much noise and too much traffic. The group felt the real reason was an anxiety to have this "strange" religious group gathering in their backyard.

They appealed to us for help. They asked if several of our clergy would come the next morning to a meeting of the Dade County Commission, which serves as an appeals forum for zoning. A few of us did attend and spoke passionately for this group's right to establish their own house of worship.

The commission voted unanimously to allow them to build their temple. Some time later, when they had the groundbreaking ceremony, they invited Shirley and me to attend. They were effusive in their praise of me and the other clergy for helping them obtain this glorious goal.

A *Miami Herald* reporter, writing an article about the event, asked me why an Orthodox rabbi would devote his efforts to help a Buddhist religion.

"To me, this was a very vital issue," I began. "For by helping secure the rights of this small religious group, I helped secure and perpetuate the rights of all religious groups, including my own."

One Saturday in February of 2003, I was on a cruise sponsored by the Miami Jewish Home and Hospital for the Aged. On that morning, I was in the middle of conducting a Sabbath service when a Protestant minister entered the room and approached me at the podium.

He whispered in my ear, "It was just announced that the shuttle Columbia broke apart upon reentry to the earth's atmosphere, killing the seven crew members, including the first Israeli astronaut, Ilan Ramon."

I immediately stopped the service and invited him to offer a prayer. As soon as the service ended, I arranged with him and the Catholic chaplain to conduct a memorial service that afternoon in the main theatre. Word quickly spread and the theatre was filled to capacity as we conducted a joint interfaith memorial service.

This emotional response helped ease the deep pain that we all shared at such a terrible loss. All of us, including the clergy, held hands as a sign that we all shared in this grief, that we are our brother's keeper, and that all of us are a part of a common humanity.

Shirley and I were invited to attend a conference in Paris during the month of March 2003. The drumbeats of war with Iraq were escalating and the animosity between France and the United States was reaching crisis proportions. This came as a result of France's opposition to the American efforts to engage in war. For security reasons, we had two motorcycle police escorts throughout our stay. This was also a time when there had been a great deal of anti-Semitic attacks on a number of Jewish institutions in France, such as the stabbing of a rabbi, the firebombing of a Jewish school, and others.

During that same mission, I had the opportunity to meet with Cardinal Jean-Marie Lustiger. The Cardinal was born a Jew and was given to a Catholic family to spare him from the Nazi onslaught against the Jews. He was raised and converted to Catholicism and subsequently moved up in the religious order to become a Cardinal. He has been a key figure in promoting Catholic-Jewish dialogue and highly revered by both communities.

With Cardinal Lustiger, who was born Jewish and
given to a Catholic family during the Holocaust,
discussing Catholic-Jewish issues in Paris, 2003

He joked with us, saying that, "It would be most
historic and ironic if he as a Jew and as a Cardinal would
be elected as Pope." He died a few years later and left
instructions that at his funeral mass, the Kaddish—a
Hebrew prayer for the dead—be recited, since he always
considered himself to be Jewish.

During our stay, Shirley had misgivings about
spending money in France, since at that time there
were very strong feelings among the French against the
United States. The mood at home was likewise very
antagonistic toward France, going so far as changing

the name of french fries to freedom fries and other similar symbolic acts.

"Maybe to show our displeasure with France," Shirley suggested. "We should boycott them and not spend any money here.'"

"Okay, if you feel that way," I said. "But when our grandchildren ask, 'Did you buy me any presents?' I'll let you be the one to answer, 'No, sweetheart, we boycotted them.'"

After thinking about it, Shirley decided that she would charge everything, at least denying them the immediate benefits of our cash.

We returned home a week before United States invaded Iraq.

In early 2007, I received a call from a woman named Portenza. She called because there was a profile of me in a South Florida magazine called *Promise*. She also had appeared in that magazine. In our conversation, she told me that she had collaborated on a book called, *Love is the Solution, Peace is Possible*. She asked me if I could read the book and send a letter endorsing it.

I agreed, but I put off writing the letter since I had other commitments. Shirley kept urging me to write the letter. Finally, I praised the book in glowing terms, since it was very well written and illustrated.

Sometime later, I received a call from Portenza.

"How would you like to go to Fiji?" she asked.

I was quite surprised and enthused by this unusual invitation, and asked her what is happening in Fiji.

"They will be hosting a world interfaith conference on peace. They are inviting 15 world religious leaders of various faiths, and you, Rabbi Schiff, should represent the Jewish faith."

Shirley and I were invited as guests of Tony Robbins, a well-known motivational speaker, who owned the Namale Resort on one of the Fiji Islands and was sponsoring this event. In my conversation with Tony, he told me that after I was recommended by Portenza, he googled me and found that I was the best fit to represent the American Jewish community at the conference.

At the opening session, each of the leaders was asked to talk about their reason for coming to the conference.

"When someone at home asked me why I was going to Fiji," I began, "I told him that my favorite apple was the Fiji, and so I will go to Fiji and bring back as many apples as I can. 'But the name of the apple is not Fiji,' my friend at home said. 'It's Fuji. It's a Fuji apple.' I responded in that moment by telling the story of a man who won the lottery by choosing the number 51. When asked by a friend why he had chosen 51, the man said, 'I have twin daughters who are 26 years old. So 26 and 26 is 51.' The friend said, 'but 26 and 26 is not 51; it is 52,' to which the man replied, 'Who won the lottery, you or me?' So, as I stood there corrected about the name of the apple, I asked my fruit critic a simple question: Who just won the lottery and is going to Fiji, you or me?"

Obviously, there was a more important reason for my accepting the invitation. It was an opportunity to meet with religious leaders of other faiths, to dialogue and to share our various core values, and to see how we can utilize those common moral and ethical values in order to promote a more peaceful world.

Another thought that I expressed during that first opening session was that, "when my life's journey ends and I arrive in Heaven, I will have had a preview here in Namale (Fiji)." A few days later, during another session, I commented that, "now that I have experienced this beautiful island, I feel that, when I finally reach Heaven, I will ask for a transfer to Namale."

As we left the island, Shirley said, "That letter you wrote was an extremely valuable one, since it brought us to this paradise, with tropical palm trees, on the golden shores of the Pacific Ocean." I totally agreed, but I also felt that the experience was even more memorable for how it had reinforced my basic belief that at the core of these various religious faith groups there lies a deep yearning for peace, respect, and love. When that yearning can be satisfied, perhaps all of us can find paradise, much as we had found it temporarily on the island of Namale. Meanwhile, I would never taste a Fuji apple quite the same way again.

Enjoying the Fiji Islands in 2007

I received a letter dated September 8, 2008, from John C. Favalora, the archbishop of Miami. The letter was to inform me that, "His Holiness Benedict XVI has bestowed upon you the Papal Medal Benemerenti. This Pontifical honor is recognition at the highest level of the Roman Catholic Church for your outstanding contribution to the Archdiocese of Miami, in promoting the common good among all the people of South Florida." The medal would be presented at St. Mary's Cathedral on the evening of Tuesday, October 7, 2008, the 50th anniversary of the establishment of Miami as an Archdiocese.

The Benemerenti medal was begun by Pope Gregory XVI in 1852, and awarded to "well deserving persons." It has rarely been awarded to persons of the Jewish faith.

The service turned out to be very inspiring. I especially appreciated the music, which included a magnificent orchestra and choir. After one of the musical renditions, someone remarked, "The Catholics sure know how to do pomp and circumstance. Tell me, Rabbi, do the Jews have pomp and circumstance?" I said, "Sometimes we have a little pomp, depending on the circumstance."

As I recollect my involvement with the Archdiocese of Miami, it seems clear to me why I received this high honor. I attended the elevation mass for the three archbishops of the Archdiocese: Coleman Carroll, Edward McCarthy, and John Favalora. I led two interfaith missions to Israel, in 1978 and in 2000, which included Archbishops McCarthy and Favalora.

The high point of the Archdiocese's 50 years was the visit to Miami by Pope John Paul II. One of the most significant events during that visit was the Pope's meeting in Miami with national Jewish leaders. And, since I had served as the liaison to the Catholic community in helping arrange this historic meeting, this must have been why the Archbishop recommended that the Pope confer upon me this award.

One extra perk from this award came most unexpectedly. Many years ago, I had been asked by a Vatican official to give my miniature Bible to the Pope in exchange for a "thank you" letter from the Pope, himself. At that time, I had politely demurred, but over the years I often wondered if I had done the right thing. My quandary was finally resolved when I received the medal from Pope Benedict XVI, with no strings attached.

One of the organizations I have been involved with since its inception in 1998 is the Interfaith Workers

Justice. I have been serving as its president for the past five years. This organization is committed to strive for the fair treatment of workers, including compensation, a safe environment, benefits, etc.

One of the issues we are involved with is trying to get employers to agree to pay their employees a "living wage." This is a pay scale considerably higher than the current minimum wage, which is now $7.25 an hour with no requirement to offer any benefits. By 2012, the "living wage" rate for employees receiving healthcare benefits should reach $11.28 an hour.

We helped pass a "living wage" ordinance in the City of Miami Beach, and in Miami–Dade County, among others. This law requires these governmental bodies to compensate their employees with a "living wage." It also requires that all contractors who do business with these governments also pay their employees a "living wage."

We also helped the janitors of the University of Miami who were on strike to get the university administration to settle their dispute and allow them to unionize. We were also instrumental in getting the Miami–Dade County Commission to pass an ordinance prohibiting "wage theft." This theft occurs when employers—mainly but not exclusively in agriculture—cheat workers by not paying them for overtime, hold back compensation indefinitely, and short change them in their compensation. These employers use all kinds of intimidations in their business practices. A considerable number of these workers are undocumented and are threfore reluctant to be whistleblowers for fear that their employer may turn them into immigration authorities.

Our organization was established as an interfaith group because respect for workers is a biblical mandate to which all faiths are committed. In the book of Leviticus (19:13), we read that, "A worker's wage shall not remain with you over night until morning." This and other biblical verses mandate that workers must not be denied their rightful compensation, but rather be treated with fairness and respect.

It is only when we practice what we preach, namely, that we utilize our efforts to bring equality and justice to workers that we live up to our religious obligations to bring justice to all. After all, what's fair is fair. This is the code of honor I adhere to and the struggle I have committed my life to on a daily basis.

Everyone blessed with long life realizes at one point or another that he or she has crossed the line into senior citizenship. I learned this once when I registered in a motel.

"Would you like to take advantage of our senior citizen discount?" the clerk asked.

This was shock number one.

I reached for my wallet to show my driver's license confirming I was eligible.

"Oh no," he said calmly. "That won't be necessary."

This was shock number two.

Shock number three is that I remember this story from so long ago!

11
Reflections

IN JANUARY 1981, I had triple bypass surgery. Shirley visited me in the hospital every afternoon after her work as a teacher. My doctors would check on me every morning.

One day, Shirley asked, "What did the doctors say today?"

I told her the doctor said, "You now have a heart of a nineteen year old."

"That's fine," Shirley said. "But don't let it go to your head."

While I was recuperating at home from my bypass surgery, one of my coworkers visited.

"My uncle had the same operation," she said.

"How did his surgery go?" I asked her, anxiously.

"It was successful," she replied.

"How long has he been living since the surgery?" I asked.

"Oh, he never survived the surgery," she said.

"How was the surgery successful," I asked, "if he didn't survive it?"

"The surgery was successful, but they couldn't get his heart started."

I turned white hearing for the first time that the doctors had stopped my heart during the surgery. I later learned that in the procedure, your heart is stopped and circulation is maintained by a heart-lung machine. Shirley wanted to strangle the woman.

As she was leaving, she said, "By the way, Rabbi, I'm sorry I didn't get to visit you before your surgery." Thank G-d she didn't, I thought, smiling at Shirley.

After leaving the hospital, I enrolled in a cardiac rehabilitation program at Mount Sinai Medical Center. Once the course was completed, they put me on a home exercise program, recommending I use a stationary bicycle like a Schwin Air-Dyne, the top of the line, which was used in the program.

When I told this to Shirley, she asked, "Why do you want such an expensive toy?"

"What do you mean, 'toy'?" I asked.

"Well, Sol," she began. "You will use it once or twice and it will be left to gather dust."

I was a little put out by this and said, "For my health, I'm going to get the best."

In retrospect, her comment was a blessing, because, after buying the eight hundred dollar bicycle, I was motivated to use it religiously, five times a week (never on Saturdays), forty minutes (ten miles) a day.

"Traveling the world" on my faithful bicycle

In 1996, eleven years after I started, I was closing in on 24,000 miles. The bicycle shop owner where I purchased it knew about my extended travels. As he was preparing to publish a brochure promoting the store's wares, he arranged to take a picture of me on the bicycle.

He asked how many miles I put on the bike and I tried to give him a cute answer.

"In about three weeks, I am going to have an around-the-world party, meaning I am going to complete 24,000 miles."

The next day, a *Miami Herald* reporter called, saying, "I heard you're having an around-the-world party. What motivated you to be so diligent in your use of the bicycle?"

I thought it wouldn't look too good in print to tell them about Shirley's initial comment when I first got the bike. Instead I said, "A friend said, 'Why buy such an expensive toy?'" I told the reporter that on January 27, the fifteenth anniversary of my surgery, I will have completed 24,000 miles, equaling the circumference of the earth, and we will have an around-the-world party.

Later in the day, the reporter said she checked and found out that the earth's circumference is 24,901 miles. I thought this revelation would kill the story. Instead, she wrote the story like this:

"The rabbi has three weeks to complete 901 miles, almost an impossibility. But knowing his zeal, I'm sure he will make it."

What had started as a cute remark suddenly had become a reality. When the story was published, we got numerous calls from people, asking us why they hadn't been invited. Shirley had no choice but to give a party. She got posters from different countries from our travel agent and prepared desserts from different countries from around the world. The guests gathered around my bicycle, as I pedaled the last half mile of my journey. The party was a rousing success and everyone wished me well on my second journey around the world. (I recently passed 58,000 miles.)

In 1968, together with a Catholic priest and a Protestant minister, I led an interfaith mission to Israel. One of my congregation Beth El members, Mrs. Spector, came to my office to ask if she could join our mission. I told her that I would welcome her participation. She then told me why she wanted to join us. Her son had been killed in World War II in Italy and he was buried there in the American Cemetery in Netuno. She carried a heavy stone in her heart because she had never visited his resting place. Now that her rabbi was traveling to Italy, it gave her the incentive to finally visit her son.

I connected with various departments in Washington, D.C., working on arrangements. A few days before the mission departed, she again came to my office with an additional feeling of guilt. For all these years, she had a gnawing feeling that her son's grave had a cross on top of it. She never pursued this, for fear of the result. Now that she was finally going to visit his grave, she would soon be faced with the reality of her suspicion, in the presence of her rabbi.

I assured her that I would do my best to research the matter. The appropriate Washington officials assured me that, if in fact the grave had a cross, they would ship a Star of David to the cemetery for installation. When I finally made contact with the right officials, they researched the issue and assured me that the grave did have a Star of David.

When I broke the news to Mrs. Spector, her sense of relief was overwhelming.

"You literally lifted a stone from my heart," she said.

Our experience was very moving and meaningful. The American officials in Washington and at the American cemetery in Netuno were extremely helpful and sensitive. A car picked us up at our hotel in Rome and drove us to the cemetery. They provided flowers and a photographer to record the ceremony. I offered appropriate prayers at the cemetery. This was really all for Mrs. Spector—the funeral nearly twenty-five years later that she never had the chance to have for her son.

With Nathan Sharansky, a famous refusnik and
now a political leader in Israel, 1995

In October 1973, right after the Yom Kippur War in Israel, my brother, Joseph, called me from New York to ask me if the name of our cousin in Israel is Feige. I said I know her as Ziporah (Hebrew for Feige). She was my father's niece and his only relative who had survived the Holocaust. She had been brought to Israel soon after its establishment. My brother told me the following story:

He got a call from a man who told him that he was in Russia. After services, outside the Moscow Synagogue, a woman approached him and said she was trying to locate her relatives in America with whom she had lost contact since the outbreak of World War II. Russian

Jews gathered regularly outside the synagogue to inquire about relatives in America. The only clues she gave were the name Rabbi Schiff and a street called Atkins in Brooklyn. The man called a few Rabbi Schiffs in the Brooklyn phone book. After a few calls, he reached my brother, Rabbi Joseph Schiff.

My brother recognized these clues. We had lived at one time on Atkins Ave. in Brooklyn and the Rabbi Schiff she was referring to was our father, Rabbi Harry Schiff. My brother wrote to this Russian woman, asking her to write about her family.

The woman wrote a letter and said, "If we are related, you will know the following story, which my mother used to tell us. Her father was a shochet, a ritual slaughterer. He used to travel from town to town, slaughtering livestock for Jewish people. One day, on one of his journeys, some hoodlums attacked him. His slaughtering knife fell to the ground. They took the knife and cut his throat and killed him."

My brother quickly recognized the story. Our father had always told us the same story about his father. We immediately realized that she was our first cousin Henya.

Soon after my brother told me this story, I was scheduled to go to Israel on a UJA mission. When I visited Ziporah we were both ecstatic about the wonderful news. Both sisters had been separated during the war and each thought the other had died. An official family reunification process was begun immediately to bring her to Israel. Happily, the sisters were soon reunited.

Our daughter-in-law, Alisa Schiff, once asked me about my work as a chaplain. I told her that I see approximately ten thousand patients a year.

"I am so impressed that you perform so many mitzvoth," she said.

"The number may be large," I said. "But the Talmud tells us that 'He who saves one life saves an entire world.' In this case, we can paraphrase, 'He who helps one person helps an entire world.'"

After the first sermon I ever gave as a rabbi, a little old lady said to me,

"Rabbi, your sermons are beautiful. You should have them published,"

to which I responded, "Maybe they will be published posthumously."

The woman replied, "Oh, I hope it will be real soon."

Acknowledgments

I WISH TO ACKNOWLEDGE several people whose help and guidance played a major role in creating this book. I must begin with my beloved wife and life partner, Shirley, who has been instrumental in every detail of this book, from its initial concept to its final proofreading. This is just one example of the fruitful results of our collaboration during our joyous journey through life.

In the two-thousand-year-old Talmudic book, *Ethics of the Fathers*, a rabbi asked his students, "What is the best quality in life that one should have?" One student said, "a good friend." Another replied, "a good neighbor." For me, Dr. Michael (Mihaly Lenart) has been both a good friend and a good neighbor. The only thing I would add to that ancient reference is "a good computer expert." His constant technical help has been invaluable. My gratitude to Michael and his wife, Dr. Ana Pasztor, for their friendship and support.

My thanks, also, to Dr. Mark Banschick, for his encouragement. Thanks to our daughter-in-law,

Dr. Jacqueline Schiff, for introducing me to Mark, who recommended David Tabatsky, the person who helped me turn my life into a book.

David started out as my editor and soon became a caring and helpful friend. Although he is not a cantor like his father was, he nevertheless is able to make words sing. His patience, unique talents, and thoughtful attention to every detail helped make this book come alive and bring my dream to a reality.

A special thanks to Jacob Solomon, President and CEO, Bonnie Reiter-Lehrer, Chief Marketing and Communications Officer, and the staff of the Greater Miami Jewish Federation; Jeffrey Freimark, President and CEO, Blaise Mercadante, Chief Marketing and Development Officer, and the staff of the Miami Jewish Health Systems; Rabbi Mark Kram, President, and Rabbi Fred Klein, Executive Vice-President of the Rabbinical Association of Greater Miami; and Steven Sonenreich, President and CEO of Mt. Sinai Medical Center.

Finally, I must mention our precious children and grandchildren: Dr. Elliot and Alisa, and their children Mikey and Brooke; Jeffrey and Risa, and their children Chananya, Moshe, and Noah; and Steven and Jacqueline and their children, Jennifer and Jeremy. I thank them all for their ongoing encouragement and love.

Sol's Leftovers

My Own Special Listening Skills

A SPEAKER ONCE ASKED those of us in attendance to close our eyes. I followed his instruction and promptly slept through the rest of the lecture. At the conclusion, the host invited three clergymen—me included—to share our reaction. I had no idea what he had said during his lecture. I thought I could get a clue from one of the other two.

The first said, "The presentation was excellent," but he spoke in generalities. No clue.

The next said, "The speaker was disappointing," and also offered no clue.

It was my turn so I began with the story of a couple that came to a rabbi to settle an argument. The husband gave his story and the rabbi said, "You are right." The wife gave her side, which was just the opposite. The rabbi said, "You are also right." The rabbi's wife asked,

"How can they both be right?" The rabbi answered, "You are right, too."

I then said that when I heard the comments of the first clergy, I thought he was right. I had the same feeling about the second. Then I mentioned that the most meaningful part of the lecture was the experiment of closing the eyes.

Later, someone told me, "You must have been the only one who listened."

Inflation

While studying at a yeshiva high school on the Lower East Side in New York, I passed a barbershop with a sign reading, "Haircut and manicure fifty cents." I had always wanted a manicure and now that I'd found a bargain, I decided to go for it. As I paid the cashier fifty cents, he said, "Where's the rest?" I said, "What do you mean?" He said, "You owe me fifty cents." I asked, "Why? The sign said haircut and manicure, fifty cents." He said, "Yes, haircut fifty cents and manicure fifty cents." I paid the extra fifty cents, feeling that I was taken.

About fifty years later, Shirley and I visited Boston for a conference. We walked through a mall, when I saw a restaurant with a sign, "Danish and coffee one dollar." I went into the restaurant and asked the cashier, "If I ordered a Danish and coffee, how much would it cost?" To which he replied, "Two dollars." I said, "The sign says, 'Danish and coffee one dollar.'" He said, "Yes, Danish a dollar and coffee a dollar." I said, "Did you ever own a barber shop?" I wondered where this fellow would open his next business.

One morning when I came to my office, a colleague observed, "I noticed that you are wearing a new pair of glasses and you have a new short haircut, and I don't like either of them." To which I responded, "My hair will grow on me, and my glasses will grow on you." You can't please everyone, especially within the politics and customs of a particular organization or congregation.

Q: With all the many assignments Moses had to accomplish in the Bible, how was he able to complete so much work?

A: He had a staff.

I took a flight to New York for a meeting. Waiting for my luggage at JFK Airport, I decided to make a phone call. After I finished the call, I walked to the carousel for my luggage. Most all of the luggage was already picked up. I noticed a little old lady wheeling my luggage away. I quickly ran to the lady, telling her it was my luggage. She argued that it was hers. While we were arguing, a young man walked in to the terminal and came over to the woman.

"Momma, what's the matter?" he asked.

"This man is trying to take away my luggage," she said.

I said, "No need to argue. We'll call over a police officer and we'll open the luggage. Then we'll see if it contains ladies or men's underwear."

"Okay, if that's your attitude," the woman said. "Here, take the luggage."

Of course, it was my luggage and it was obvious that the mistaken luggage was a scam. I said at that time that there should be a security person checking each person's claim check to avoid such pilfering. Soon after, this format was instituted in all airports. Before this security system was established, one could say, "Crime does pay."

Dressed as Nero fiddling around with Cleopatra while
Rome burned, Shirley and I won first prize in a costume
contest on the NCL cruise ship M.S. *Skyward* in 1973

There is a story of two Jewish men who came from
Europe and started a small business. Their names were
Goldberg and Cohen. Their business succeeded beyond
expectations. They reached the highest level of success
and became a Fortune 500 company. They hired a top
P.R. firm to develop a high-class image. The specialist
suggested that the name Goldberg and Cohen is not
fitting for such an elite firm. He suggested a prominent
American name, "McKinley & McKinley."

On the first day using this new name, someone
called the company and asked, "May I speak with Mr.

McKinley?" To which the receptionist answered, "Which one, Goldberg or Cohen?"

In the winter of 2007, Shirley and I stopped in Las Vegas on the way back from a convention in Los Angeles. When we arrived at the hotel, there were hawkers roaming the lobby trying to sell timeshares. One of them caught my attention. She offered us two free tickets to the most popular play on the Strip, *Mamma Mia*. The condition for the gift was that we had to listen to a presentation concerning a timeshare offer. We figured that since we are not going to buy anything it is an easy investment in order to get free tickets to a popular play. This was a big mistake!

The next morning, we were hustled onto a bus, together with many other hostages—I mean participants—and driven to a meeting place somewhere in the desert. They served lunch at no charge, which we did not eat since it was not kosher.

A salesman sat us down and began talking to us about the great opportunity to own a vacation pad for two weeks a year, forever. And the price, he said, was only $32,000. Shirley thought it was a bargain and suggested that we should accept the offer.

I stuck to my guns and told him, "We are not interested." I suggested that we would go back to Miami and think it over. He responded by saying, "Once you leave here, the offer is withdrawn." He kept pushing, and I kept saying "no" over and over for about forty-five minutes.

He then called over his supervisor to better explain the deal. The supervisor was a very smooth talker who lauded the great opportunity. He offered us the time-share for $22,000.

Shirley said, "Let's take it, we already saved ten thousand dollars."

I said to this new hustler, "I know that the deal is off if I leave Las Vegas. However, can I call my lawyer to discuss this matter with him?"

"No, you can't call him," he said.

"Even a prisoner is entitled to one phone call," I said.

"Those are the rules," he replied.

After each of the pitchmen, I said, "Please give me my free tickets and 'let my people go.'" Their answer was, always, "Yes, we will give you the tickets but we want you to see the full picture."

After going round and round on the same subject and getting more and more annoyed, I finally said, "Listen, I paid my dues, and did my time. Now I insist on getting my tickets as promised."

"Okay," the supervisor responded. "I will take you to the person who gives the tickets."

He took us into another room, where he introduced us to the manager who assured us that she would give us the tickets. But instead of giving us tickets she gave us another pitch.

"By the way, did they show you the timeshare apartment?" she asked.

"No, they didn't." I said.

"That was a mistake," she replied. "Because they failed to show you the apartment, I will lower the price to nine thousand nine hundred dollars."

At this point, we realized that if it sounds too good to be true, it is. Since they finally ran out of pitchmen, she reluctantly gave us our tickets.

There is a well-known line that goes like this: "Besides that, how was the play, Mrs. Lincoln?" And by the way, *Mamma Mia* was great but hardly worth the time and aggravation. I should have paid for the tickets in the first place. On top of that, this was perfect proof that there is no free lunch.

In October 2010, the Dalai Lama was a guest speaker at a multifaith program at Temple Emanu-El on Miami Beach. After the program ended, a Catholic priest (Father Pat O'Neil) attempted to snap a picture of the Dalai Lama and me. The priest had trouble snapping the picture. Instead of pressing the snap button, he kept pressing the zoom button. Tension was rising as hundreds eagerly awaited a fleeting meet-and-greet with the Dalai Lama. Finally, after what seemed like forever, the Dalai Lama said to the priest, "You need to have some training in snapping pictures." He proceeded to point to the snap button. The priest finally succeeded in taking the picture, to the great relief of the audience.

It took a Tibetan monk to solve a **tri**-faith "crisis."

The moral of the story is, if at first you don't succeed, **tri tri** again.

With the Dalai Lama in Miami Beach, 2010, at an international interfaith symposium

I once read that the Colgate-Palmolive Company was planning to market a toothpaste product in the Far East named "Darkie." In February 1986, I wrote a letter to the president of the company, urging him to change the name, "since the term Darkie has negative racial connotations."

The company responded to my letter, informing me that the name Darkie has been used in that area for more than sixty years. The packaging includes a likeness of the famous Al Jolson—in his minstrel outfit—and that no offense was intended. The letter clearly indicated that no name change would take place.

However, in a later letter, dated January 31, 1989, S.M. Ford, executive vice president of Colgate-Palmolive, informed me that, "after extensive negotiations, we have decided to change the name and the graphics on the package."

In an enclosed corporate statement, the company stated that Colgate-Palmolive has agreed that the old name (Darkie) and package presentation represented offensive racial stereotyping that should be changed.

"The name Darkie will be changed to Darlie," they wrote. "In addition, the caricature of a minstrel in black face on the current package will be changed to a non-racially offensive silhouette."

The letter concluded with: "Given your interest, this letter is to let you know that action has been taken, and to thank you for writing our company."

Two conclusions can be derived from this incident. First, one should never remain silent in the face of wrongdoing. Second, one should never underestimate the ability to influence powerful establishments when logic and reason are brought to their attention.

That's the Way the Ball Bounces

As part of Jewish Heritage Day on April 3, 2011, I was invited to participate in the ceremony before the Florida Marlins faced the New York Mets. When I met Rabbi Roni Raab, the principal of the Hebrew Academy of Miami Beach who had coordinated the event, I thanked him for giving me enough notice, so that I could prepare my speech.

"Oh no, Sol," he said, smiling. "This is not a talking gig; it's a throwing gig."

After I threw out the ceremonial first pitch and was heading back to my seat, I ran into one of the players.

"The ball I threw, was it a ball or a strike?"

"I couldn't really tell, sir," he replied. "You see, it hit the ground before it reached the catcher."

I was given the ball in a case as a souvenir.

Someone asked, "Did they also give you a glove?"

"No," I said, "but they told me, 'The ball we gave you will fit into any glove you buy.'"

My fun "under the yarmulke" never ends!

With my new friends at the Marlins' game,
where I threw out the first pitch

Most of our family joined Shirley and I when we
were honored by the Rabbi Alexander S. Gross
Hebrew Academy on Miami Beach in 1999

Gems from my Grandchildren

TOLD SOMEONE at my office that my grandson Moshe was born today, October 31, 1997.

"Will his parents call him their Halloween baby?" she asked.

I said, "Not a ghost of a chance, since they are observant and Halloween is certainly not a Jewish holiday."

When I told this to my daughter-in-law Risa, she said, "But we do call him our little pumpkin."

I gave a prayer for the U.S. Senate on July 29, 1999, and we rushed back from Washington, D.C., to attend the Bris (the circumcision ceremony) of our grandson Jeremy Moshe in Stamford, Connecticut. We were traveling in the van of our children, Elliot and Alisa, and their children, Mikey and Brooke. I was sitting next to Brooke, age four. She began to whine.

"I'm thirsty. I want a drink."

To pacify her, I said, "Sweetheart, when we get to the party, you will have all kinds of drinks. What is your favorite?"

She said, "Coca-Cola."

"Good," I said. "Because you own a share of Coca-Cola."

"No!" she declared. "I'm not going to share my Coca-Cola with anyone."

One Friday, I observed our fourteen-year-old grand-daughter Jennifer helping her mother light the Sabbath candles before sundown. It is customary for the mother of the house to light the candles. Generally, a woman begins to observe that ritual as soon as she gets married.

"You are starting to light candles very early," I said to Jennifer. "By the time you get married, you will be able to say the prayers with your eyes closed."

(During the candle lighting ceremony, the woman usually covers her eyes.)

To which Jennifer replied, "That's how I already do it. I perform the lighting ceremony with my eyes closed."

While doing some construction in our house, we replaced three small closets with one large walk-in closet. This left a large blank wall facing our living room. One day, our grandson Chananya looked at the wall and suggested that I place all my framed photographs on it.

As he helped me so nicely he asked, "Zaidie, how did you get to be in pictures with five American presidents and so many other important people?"

"Sweetheart," I replied. "They all happened to be in the right place at the right time."

My grandchild Moshe once asked me, "Zaidie, how do you remember all of your jokes?"

"I have a chip in my head," I told him. "And all my jokes are on it."

"How can I remember all of your jokes?" he asked.

I said, "You'll have to get a chip off the old block."

For more information and features,
please visit
www.undertheyarmulke.com

Made in the USA
Charleston, SC
12 January 2012